GW00372914

Jack Altman

JPM Publications

Contents

This Way Cuba   3

Flashback   7

On the Scene   17

   Havana   17

   The Northwest   35

   The Centre   42

   The East   49

   Isla de la Juventud   57

   and Los Cayos

Cultural Notes   60

Shopping   65

Dining Out   67

Nightlife   70

Sports   74

The Hard Facts   76

Index   80

Fold-out maps

  Cuba, Havana

  Old and Central Havana

  Santiago de Cuba

▌*Photo page 1: Cienfuegos*

This Way Cuba

More than Swaying Palms

Here is one Caribbean island where you would not want to spend all your time on the beach. The people are bright, self-assertive and handsome. Their cultural heritage is colourful, as are the monuments of their often tumultuous, always fascinating, history. The country has evolved with a strong personality from its experience of Spanish colonialism, slavery, civil war, invasion, revolution and relentless economic blockade. Havana, the island's proud capital, is energetically restoring the buildings of its elegant historic quarters, and the grand old cities of Santiago de Cuba and Trinidad still recall their 16th-century beginnings.

Don't worry, Cuba lacks none of the classical Caribbean attractions. The beaches *are* splendid, nearly 300 of them, many with fine white sands and almost all of them gloriously unspoiled. They are ideal for water sports—scuba-diving, fishing and sailing—well catered for with first-class hotels in modern resort towns like Varadero and Guardalavaca. Go hiking or horseback riding in the interior and you will see the palm trees and other sub-tropical flora in their green plenty in a land-scape alternating rugged mountains with pleasant valleys and farmland. The resorts do ample justice to Cuba's tangy Caribbean cuisine—good seafood, great beach barbecues, luscious fruit—not forgetting those famous rum cocktails.

Lie of the Land

Cuba is the biggest island in the Caribbean, almost as big as all the others put together. It stands at the entrance to the Gulf of Mexico, its western end only 145 km (90 miles) from Florida's Key West. Haiti is even closer, 77 km (48 miles) to the east across the Windward Passage. The island extends some 1,300 km (over 800 miles) in length. At its widest point, it measures about 200 km (124 miles), and at its narrowest, just 35 km (22 miles) across. Cuba comprises an archipelago of around 1,600 isles and *cayos* (cays), the largest being the Isla de la Juventud (Isle of Youth) south of Batabanó Bay. Sheltered by long coral reefs, the coastal beaches face the Bahamas and Atlantic Ocean to the northeast, Jamaica and the Caribbean Sea to the south.

Three mountainous regions account for more than a third of 3 the total land mass. In the southeastern Oriente region, the Sierra Maestra range, extending from Cabo Cruz to Guantánamo, is rich in flora and fauna and includes the island's highest mountain, Pico Turquino, alt. 1,972 m (6,470 ft). East of Santiago de Cuba and Guantánamo (where the US Navy still has its military base), the peaks and ridges of Gran Piedra, Boniato and Purial, deeply dissected by streams, rise inland from the coast like massive granite steps.

In the central province of Las Villas, the lower Guamuhaya range (or Sierra del Escambray), between 1,160 m (3,800 ft) and 850 m (2,800 ft), is divided by the Agabama river. Its slopes are notable for the coffee plantations and several lakes.

At the western end of the island, in the Havana and Pinar del Río provinces, is the tobacco and rice country of the Guaniguanico mountains, comprising the Sierra del Rosario and Sierra de los Órganos.

Between these ranges is a countryside of gently rolling hills and lowlands where the vital sugar crop is harvested and cattle herds graze, notably on the broad plains of Camagüey. Of the island's 200 rivers, the longest and most navigable are the Cauto in Oriente, flowing parallel to the Sierra Maestra north into the Gulf of Guacanayabo, and the Sagua la Grande flowing north from the Guamuhaya mountains down to the port of La Isabela.

The Island's Riches

The flora numbers no less than 8,000 varieties. Dense sub-tropical forests cover the humid lower mountain slopes, providing valuable timber products. Woods on the higher, drier slopes are principally pine and eucalyptus. The island boasts an astonishing assortment of palm trees, the best known being the royal palm, indigenous to Cuba.

Sugar and its derivatives are the principal source of revenue, followed by tobacco, the Cuban cigar still being the most sought after in the world—and favourite contraband into the United States. Other sources are cattle breeding and fisheries, while agricultural products include rice, beans, coffee, maize and fruit.

Sunny Weather

Thanks to the warm waters of the Gulf Stream and the trade winds (northeast in the summer, southeast in winter), the island's climate is moderate and stable, sub-tropical but less hot than elsewhere in the Caribbean. In Havana, the average temperature hovers around 25°C (77°F). The dry season lasts from November to mid-May and the rainy season from mid-May to October, but even then, Havana, Santiago de Cuba, Varadero and the other beach resorts rarely have more than two consecutive days of rain. If they come at all, hurricanes blow into the Caribbean from June to November—150 recorded in the 500 years after Christopher Columbus nearly lost his fleet. Since then, Cuba has installed an excellent early-warning system. The worst storms usually arrive in September and October, blowing torrential rain with winds of up to 250 km an hour (nearly 160 mph).

The People
The island's population is close to 11,000,000, a fifth of them living in Havana, the largest city in the Caribbean—in addition to some 700,000 exiles, mostly in Miami. Other major cities are Santiago de Cuba (440,100), Camagüey (294,000) and Holguín (242,100). According to official census figures, 70 per cent of Cubans are white, 12 per cent black, most of them in Oriente province, and 17 per cent mixed (*mestizo* and mulatto). It is generally agreed, however, that the percentage of "mixed blood" is much higher, perhaps as much as half the population. (The island's Caribbean Indians were almost totally wiped out under Spanish colonization.) At any

rate, the blend of Spanish and African has produced men and women of often quite stunning good looks, lithe and graceful.

The island's Catholic community, 85 per cent of the population before the 1959 revolution, is making a comeback, especially since the Pope's visit in 1998, though they still number fewer than 40 per cent. More popular are the Afro-Cuban *santería* cults blending West African Yoruba rituals with references to Catholic saints and the Virgin Mary.

The Sound of Music
Even when music isn't pouring out of a cassette recorder on the balcony, Afro-Cuban rhythms seem to punctuate conversation and even moments of silence, when the islanders may start to sway their shoulders and hips or shuffle their feet to the imagined beat of a salsa, mambo, rumba or cha-cha-chá. If Mexico and Brazil are the Cubans' favourite Latin American countries, it's because of the shared taste for their music, drawing on Spanish, African and distant, but never entirely lost, American Indian roots. Even when life is at its toughest, the Cubans find time for a party in a backyard or down at the beach—and happily invite curious passers-by, who make themselves even more welcome when they bring a bottle of rum. 5

Beginnings

From its earliest days, people from North and South America found Cuba an inviting target. The island attracted prehistoric settlers from all directions. They came in via the Bahamas and the Florida Keys, from the Caribbean coasts of Honduras and Nicaragua via Jamaica, or island-hopping from the delta of Venezuela's Orinoco river via Haiti.

Around 1000 BC, Ciboney Indians occupied the central and western half of the island, hunting and fishing. These small semi-nomadic clans lived in simple thatched beach huts or caves in cliffs and ravines.

The Arawaks (also known as Taíno Indians) arrived in the 9th century AD, moving north along the West Indian archipelago from South America to escape the fierce Carib Indians. After they in turn drove the Ciboney to the western part of the island, the Arawaks set to farming Cuba's fertile upland interior.

Cuba Discovers the Spanish

Christopher Columbus disembarked on October 28, 1492, somewhere between Gibara and Guardalavaca. Following threats of mutiny and an overnight rainstorm, he wrote with undisguised relief in his journal: "Everything I saw was so lovely that my eyes could not weary beholding such beauty." The first contact with the Arawaks was friendly. Columbus admired their tent-shaped houses, swept clean inside, with well-arranged furniture fashioned from palm branches. He watched them spinning and weaving cotton, and noted an already well-entrenched *machismo*: "It appears to me that the women work more than do the men." A second trip along the south coast at the end of 1493 failed to turn up the desired gold, but convinced Columbus and his officers to sign an affidavit that Cuba was a peninsula of the Asian mainland.

The Spanish began colonizing Cuba in earnest only after 1508, when feuds at Santo Domingo, rebellious Indians and dwindling resources drove landowner Diego Velázquez to seek fresh territories. With other settlers coming in from Jamaica, seven towns were founded between 1512 and 1515: Baracoa, Bayamo, Sancti Spíritus, Havana, Trinidad, Puerto Príncipe (now Camagüey) and Santiago de Cuba, the capital.

The Indians' resistance to this expropriation of their island was 7 broken by a four-month campaign of massacre and pillage. Spanish herding and cattle breeding upset the island's ecological balance. Animals replaced indigenous humans in the interior as pigs, goats, sheep, horses and mules ran wild through the Indians' crops and grazed the natural grasslands. From a population estimated to have been 112,000 when the Spanish arrived, the Indians were reduced to under 3,000 in the 1550s. They were wiped out by famine, disease and malnutrition. As a last desperate act of protest, many resorted to mass suicide. In the eastern mountains, small bands of rebels staged guerrilla warfare, mainly in the Sierra Maestra, that perpetual focus of Cuban revolt.

Gold was found only in small amounts in the riverbeds of central uplands and around Trinidad, Sancti Spíritu and Bayamo. Maritime activity moved westwards to Mexico and the Yucatan Peninsula, while Havana expanded and gradually superseded Santiago.

In the 1550s, Cuba took on a new role as Caribbean kingpin in the outer defence perimeter of the Spanish empire. The island was vital to protection of Spain's two annual fleets from repeated assaults by French, British and Dutch pirates. It provided meat and leather from its cattle and excellent shipping timber from its forests. By 1600, Havana had built three new fortresses. The naval port soon bustled with the classical riffraff of peddlers, gamblers, deserters, criminals and prostitutes (Indian and African slaves). Since only government officials and senior army officers were accompanied by European women, the slaves also served as concubines on the plantations, mothering the island's first generation of Creoles.

Smugglers, Planters and Slaves

By the time Havana was formally declared capital in 1607, Cuba's identity—*Cubanidad*—had already split in two, ruling classes and rebels, divided geographically. With half of the island's total 20,000 population, Havana dominated the western region's officialdom, landowners and planters of tobacco and sugar cane. In the eastern region—Oriente—the maverick population of smaller traders dealt in contraband traffic with the Portuguese, British, Dutch and French.

In the first half of the 18th century, Spain's Bourbon dynasty imposed a royal monopoly on trade. This sought to stop local manufacture and limit Cuba to exporting raw materials and importing textiles, foodstuffs and manufactured goods from Spain at highly inflated prices. Smuggling soared, notably in tobacco, of which 75 per cent of Cuba's world exports were contraband. In 1717, some 500 anti-monopoly tobacco farmers (*vegueros*) marched into Havana and forced the resignation of the governor-general. Military reprisals drove the *vegueros* to migrate and found what became some of the world's best tobacco plantations around Piñar del Río—originally producing only contraband crops.

Spain's intervention in the Seven Years War (1756–63) provoked the British occupation of Havana in 1762. This opened Cuba up to world trade. Instead of just 15 ships a year, over 1,000 vessels streamed into Havana harbour. After Spain swapped Florida for Havana, the economically more liberal Bourbon regime of Charles III welcomed British and North American merchants and dealers with consumer goods, sugar machinery for local production—and slaves.

During the ten months of British occupation, 10,000 African slaves had arrived on the island, as many as in the previous ten years, and another 50,000 came in by the end of the century. This rapid influx accompanied an increasing emphasis on sugar production. It also served to cement relations with the recently independent neighbour, the USA.

Cuba's Spanish ruling classes admired a country where progressive ideals of democracy co-existed with slavery on labour-intensive plantations.

"Wars of Liberation"

When Madrid threatened to bow to British pressure to abolish slavery in the 1820s, planters called for annexation to the USA. The campaign was halted by the American Civil War and Emancipation Proclamation of 1863. Slave-prices shot up to 1,500 pesos (from 300 pesos in 1800).

Creole property owners were in constant conflict with the Spanish élite (*peninsulares*) dominating Cuban government and finance. In 1868, after Madrid had systematically rejected their Reformist Party's demands for change, sugar planters in Oriente and the cattle barons of Camagüey raised a rebel army of 40,000 whites and blacks. In the ensuing Ten Years War, the moderate aims of the patrician Creoles gave way to the more radical demands of poorer whites and blacks for an outright end to Spanish rule and slavery. To stop the revolt reaching the rich western plantations, the Spanish army built a fortified ditch across Camagüey and brought in reinforcements. In 1878, weakened by dissent and desertions, the rebel army accepted a pact promising 9 the abolition of slavery and limited political reforms.

Slavery ended in 1886, but the seeds of renewed turbulence remained. US investors gradually edged out Spain as controlling force in the island's economy. Cuban planters abandoned production to become American-employed farmers. By 1894, the US market accounted for 90 per cent of Cuba's exports and provided 40 per cent of its imports. A new liberal Autonomist party pressed for the promised reforms without demanding independence. Conservative *peninsulares* refused all concessions. Cuban exiles, some 100,000 in Latin America, the USA and Europe, promoted *Cuba Libre*—separation from Spain *and* the USA.

Their most eloquent leader, José Martí (1853–95) was, like many Cuban revolutionaries, a freemason who sought social as well as political revolution, a Cuba free of racism and oppression. The Havana-born son of *peninsulares* formed a coalition of peasants, blacks, petit bourgeois Creoles, impoverished gentry and proletariat. From his base in the USA in 1895, the poet and journalist landed with General Máximo Gómez at Baracoa, met up with the dissident forces of Antonio Maceo and launched a new assault on the Spanish regime. Martí was killed in an early battle, but what the Spanish had perceived as just another provincial uprising soon turned into full-scale war. For the first time, the rebels crossed from Oriente into the prosperous western half of the island, recruiting thousands of peasants as they went. By January 1896, Maceo was in Pinar del Río and Gómez near Havana.

The Spanish brought in 50,000 new troops. Under their ruthless general, Valeriano Weyler, they herded 300,000 men, women and children into camps of *reconcentración*. But the insurgents continued their advance.

Faced with the threat of Cuban independence, the USA declared war on the Spanish in April 1898. Overwhelming American forces blockaded the Spanish fleet at Santiago de Cuba but had a hard time forcing a surrender. At San Juan Hill, where 700 Spanish defenders were holding off 6,000 US troops, Theodore Roosevelt led his Rough Riders on a legendary charge that caused heavy American casualties but carried Teddy into the White House.

The New Republic

In the Paris treaty of December 1898 ending the Spanish-American War, the USA stopped short of annexing Cuba along with Puerto Rico, the Philippines and Guam, but imposed economic and political control of the new republic. In enlightened colonial style, the Americans improved schools, public works and public health facilities, but they also took command of mining, sugar and other agricultural production—and leased a permanent naval base at Guantánamo Bay.

US military advisors setting up a new Cuban artillery corps stipulated that "all officers will be white". To keep their traditional hold on the black vote, the island's Liberal rulers clamped down on the fledgling black political party, *Agrupación Independiente de Color*. In 1912, a revolt in Oriente ended with hundreds of blacks being killed.

The new Cuban rulers devoted much of their limited power to amassing personal fortunes through corruption in government and public office. The 1920s were a boom-and-bust era as sugar prices soared and plummeted. Reformist Liberals pushed for new industry and agricultural diversification, but they were too late to stave off bankruptcies and mass unemployment. After a general strike and student and peasant demonstrations, reform under Gerardo Machado gave way to state terror through secret police and death-squads.

Women's groups, liberal professionals, professors and students staged guerrilla warfare against the Machado dictatorship.

US envoy Sumner Welles arrived in 1933 to conduct "friendly mediation" and force Machado's replacement by a "safe" moderate. In the course of a Cuban Army mutiny under Sergeant Fulgencio Batista for better pay—the "Sergeants' Coup"—a progressive liberal putsch brought in a junta which enacted sweeping land and labour reforms. With American interests under threat, Welles encouraged Batista to throw army support to the junta's opposition. From 1934, Batista ruled Cuba, at first through puppet presidents, then taking direct control in 1940 with a Populist image as defender of *"los humildes"* (the humble ones).

In World War II, the US consolidated its grip on the economy with the collapse of European markets. After the war, a "reformist" interlude degenerated, once more, into the graft and corruption of which the progressives had accused Batista. He swept back into power in 1952 with a military coup that substituted martial law for the constitution. Batista used government funds to buy off the unions, the press and the Catholic Church. Turning away from the Communists in these Cold War years, he found new friends in the Mafia. US organized crime ran Havana's drug traffic, gambling casinos, brothels and some of its most

11

A SPECIAL PAPA

He first came to the island in 1928—just for two weeks. The idea was to do a little deep-sea fishing, catch a couple of swordfish. He stayed at the Ambos Mundos, a hotel on Obispo, corner of Mercaderes. The room he rented on the 5th floor was not much, scarcely more than a bed. True, he did have a great view of the cathedral and the entrance to the harbour.

Day after day, he confronted the sea, sharing the life of the fishermen. The two weeks went. He stayed. Two months. Havana began to grow on him. He liked Calle Obispo, it was busy. He left and soon returned, again and again. He stayed, for longer periods, always in the Ambos Mundos, room 511. He started writing *For Whom the Bell Tolls* there.

In 1939, he bought a house in the Havana suburb of San Francisco de Paula. But he returned regularly to the downtown bar of El Floridita (Obispo 557). The daiquiris he ordered had a double shot of rum, the famous *Papa's Special*. A favourite pastime was beating his own drinking record. The challenge was tough, but he managed it.

People also claim to remember him at the Bodeguita del Medio, the corner bar that opened near the Ambos Mundos in the 40s. That was where he came for one last drink: a *mojito*—white rum flavoured with lemon and fresh mint, the bar-owner's special concoction. He liked that bar.

It was his days in Havana which inspired him to write *To Have and Have Not*, the story of an American smuggler riding the crest of the Cuban waves. His *Old Man and the Sea* clinched the Nobel Prize for him in 1954 and immortalized the fishing village of Cojímar, east of Havana.

Hemingway—yes, that's the guy—spent a third of his life in Cuba, an island he cherished as much as he cherished the Cubans. It was mutual. He is part of their collective memory now. His ghost hangs around the cafés, the bars, the restaurants and, most movingly of all, his sprawling home, *Finca Vigía*.

When he left the island for good in 1960, he left his house to the Cuban government, which turned it into a museum. All the everyday paraphernalia of the writer is still there. The atmosphere is such that some people would not be surprised to see the great man lurch in through the doorway, carrying one of his favourite cats—and a glass in his hand. Others know: no chance. Papa hated museums.

respectable hotels. The Cuban capital boasted more Cadillacs than any city in America.

The Revolution

On July 26, 1953, Fidel Castro, a 27-year-old lawyer, led an abortive attack on Moncada Barracks in Santiago de Cuba. His trial defence statement became the manifesto of the Cuban revolution, "History Will Absolve Me". Granted an amnesty in 1955 and exiled to Mexico, he organized the July 26 Movement with his brother Raúl and an Argentine doctor, Ernesto "Che" Guevara.

Of the band of 82 revolutionaries that landed in the *Granma* motor launch on an Oriente beach in December 1956, barely a dozen escaped with Fidel, Raúl and Che to the Sierra Maestra mountains to organize guerrilla warfare. Stirred by Castro's fiery rhetoric, hundreds of peasants were recruited by the *Fidelistas* to attack Rural Guard outposts. Batista retaliated by relocating rural families in detention camps in Santiago de Cuba and Bayamo. Castro recalled in his tracts the Spaniards' *reconcentración* camps in 1896 and adopted the old insurgent tactic of burning the big land-owners' sugar crops. His slogan rang "Either Batista without the *zafra* (sugar harvest) or the *zafra* without Batista." Che's urban guerrillas carried out large-scale sabotage with bombs and fires, cut power-lines and derailed trains.

The Cuban Communist Party did not support Castro until mid-1958 when victory seemed possible. Batista's 1958 summer offensive—12,000 troops in the Sierra Maestra backed by naval and air force bombardments—collapsed amid widespread desertions and defections. After a key victory by Che Guevara's *barbudos* (bearded guerrilla fighters) at Santa Clara, the insurrectionist counter-attack swept westwards through the major agricultural holdings towards Havana. As the US desperately sought an anti-Castro alternative to Batista, a military coup forced the dictator to flee to the Dominican Republic with $40 million of government funds. A general strike forced the military junta to hand over power to the July 26 Movement; Fidel arrived in Havana on January 8, 1959. A month later, he was prime minister.

In lightning succession, Fidel Castro pushed through over 1,500 decrees, laws and edicts to promote health, education, unemployment relief, to raise wages, cut rents by half, reduce costs for telephone, electricity and water, and stop imports of 200 luxury items, including Cadillacs. Other laws ended discrimination against Afro-Cubans in jobs, schools,

Throughout the island, Che Guevara is still revered as a national hero.

landownership and access to hotels and beaches. Agrarian reforms expropriated landowners and redistributed the land. Furious, the US government declared that without "prompt, adequate and effective compensation", it would end its sugar import quota.

Castro imposed his will through charisma, rousing oratory, personal heroism, moral authority and sheer energy. His embrace of Communism was largely dictated by political necessity, the implementation of his reforms, and the need for an alternative to the USA. In the face of his authoritarian style, liberals left the government and the Cuban

Communist Party became an essential ally. Soviet, East German and Polish trade delegations arrived in early 1960, providing new markets for Cuban sugar. The Soviet Union offered cheap oil; when Cuban-based American companies refused to refine it, Cuba nationalized their holdings. In rapid tit for tat, the US stopped all sugar imports, Cuba expropriated banks, telephone, electricity, railway and sugar companies, and the US imposed a trade embargo.

On President Eisenhower's orders, the CIA was arming and training Cuban émigrés in Florida and Central America. In April 1961, Kennedy inherited their plan to invade the south coast's Bahía de Cochinos, the Bay of Pigs. Fidel took personal charge of the forces that stopped the invasion in 72 hours. Some 200 of the 1,400 Cuban exiles were killed, the rest captured and eventually ransomed back to the USA.

In October 1962, however, the limits of the Soviet Union's commitment to Cuba were revealed when, without consulting Castro, it bowed to US pressure to withdraw its nuclear missiles from the island. Castro responded to Soviet "betrayal" with an independent policy of supporting similar revolutions in Latin America and Africa. But in 1967, the death of Che Guevara while leading rebel forces in the Bolivian jungle halted the revolutionary campaign *(Vía Insurreccional),* and harsh economic realities pulled Cuba back into line. The Soviet Union had cut 20 per cent off oil deliveries and increased exports to Brazil and Chile, both hostile to Cuba. When Cuba sent troops to Syria, Angola and Ethiopia in the 1970s, it was with Soviet approval.

The island's achievements in health and education (one of the world's highest adult literacy rates, superior to the USA) have been spectacular, despite the massive exodus of the Cuban élite. For the government, this emigration was at least a relatively cost-effective way of eliminating political opposition.

Cuba's economy fell victim to the US trade embargo, the over-centralized Soviet model of Marxism and the final collapse of the Soviet empire. Industry and public transportation were crippled through lack of spare parts for the US-built vehicles and machinery. Tightening of the American economic blockade cut medicines, food and basic supplies to a bare minimum. But however increasingly disillusioned the majority might be, Castro continued to put his faith in the people's powerful sense of national identity. Billboards throughout the island still loudly proclaimed in 1998: *Todo por la patría.*

To break out of the stranglehold and isolation imposed by the blockade, Castro began to court the Catholic Church. In 1997, Christmas was reinstated as a public holiday for the first time since 1970, when it was abolished, said Fidel, to enable people to achieve sugar quotas. On his momentous mission to Cuba in January 1998, Pope John Paul II preached the Christian word and championed human rights, but also criticized the US embargo. It was the signal for the last Latin American hold-outs to resume diplomatic relations with Cuba. Things were looking up.

On the Scene

Our sightseeing section divides the island into five parts, starting in Havana. The West couples Cuba's top beach resort of Varadero with the Pinar del Río tobacco country. In the Centre, see Cienfuegos, with its charming neoclassical French touch and the old Spanish colonial towns of Trinidad and Camagüey. The historic eastern region includes Santiago de Cuba, the Sierra Maestra mountains, and the Guardalavaca beach resort on the north coast. Finally, we visit the luxury island-resorts of Cayo Largo, Cayo Coco and Guillermo, and the bigger, more popular Isla de la Juventud.

HAVANA
Old Havana, City Centre, Malecón, Vedado, City Outskirts

The city, with a population of 2,180,000 the biggest in the Caribbean, mirrors all phases of the island's turbulent story. Nowhere in Latin America will you find more handsome buildings from the Spanish colonial era. Palaces, mansions and churches are being painstakingly conserved in the old quarter, La Habana Vieja (a UNESCO World Heritage Site since 1982), along with fortresses around the harbour. Garish evidence of the US presence in Cuban history is there in the grand old 50s Chevrolets and Cadillacs miraculously still rolling through the streets—and in the Vedado district's hotels that were headquarters for the Mafia's nightclubs and casinos. And monuments of the Cuban Revolution abound on and around the Plaza de la Revolución where Fidel Castro roused the people with his fiery marathon speeches. Equally present are the ghosts of past heroes like the poet of Cuban independence, José Martí, and the island's best-loved American, Ernest Hemingway.

A glimpse of the Capitolio Nacional in Central Havana, now the Academy of Sciences.

17

Old Havana

The historical core of the capital commands the entrance to the sheltered harbour that made the city's fortune. It grew out of the settlement first known as San Cristóbal de La Habana, relocated here from the southern coast in 1519.

Plaza de Armas

The square on Old Havana's eastern edge is a natural gateway to any walking tour. The plaza assembled the firepower that carried out the city's principal task in the 16th century, protecting the Spanish treasure fleets coming in and out of the Caribbean.

On the north side of the square, the massive Castillo de la Real Fuerza is the oldest surviving fortress in the Americas, rebuilt in 1558 after a French pirate attack. Notice, on its western

tower, the Giraldilla, a landmark bronze weathervane popularly believed to represent the wife of Hernando de Soto, conquistador and early governor of Cuba—the original (17th-century) is in the municipal museum across the square. Now housing the Museo de la Cerámica Artística Cubana, with a fine view of the harbour from an upstairs bar, the castle served as residence for the Spanish military commanders for 200 years.

They moved to the grand Palacio de los Capitanes Generales on the west side of the square in 1791. After the last of the commanders left in 1898, the city's finest piece of baroque architecture became, successively, headquarters for the US military governors, Cuba's first presidential palace and the Havana Town Hall until it was finally transformed, in

HIGHLIGHTS OF HAVANA

- **Catedral de San Cristóbal de La Habana**—jewel of Habana Vieja
- **Palacio de los Capitanes Generales**—city's finest baroque building, now municipal museum
- **La Bodeguita del Medio**—bar where Hemingway drank his mojito nightcaps
- **Malecón**—seafront promenade for young lovers and old fishermen
- **Plaza de la Revolución**—shrine of Cuban Revolution where Castro delivered his most fiery speeches
- **El Morro**—16th-century fortress, for a great view of the harbour

NO BLARNEY IN HAVANA

The popular O'Reilly Street leading west from Plaza de Armas bears the name not of an Irish revolutionary, but of Alejandro O'Reilly, Cuba's Governor General in 1764. As Spanish as the good men of neighbouring Obispo and Obrapía, O'Reilly earned the islanders' admiration for defending them against the commercial exploitation of the crown of Spain.

1968, into the city museum (Museo de la Ciudad). With vivid oil paintings and memorabilia of war heroes, the museum traces the town's history and the island's campaigns for independence. The statue of Columbus in the courtyard was erected in 1862.

In the middle of the plaza stands a marble statue of Carlos Manuel de Céspedes, a leader of the independence movement in the Ten Years' War (1868–78). A second-hand book market is held here at the weekend.

Two other impressive baroque edifices grace the plaza: on the northwest corner, the 18th-century Palacio del Segundo Cabo was the Spanish vice-governor's residence and is now home to the Cuban Book Institute; the Palacio de los Condes de Santovenia has been converted into the luxury Hotel Santa Isabel.

On the east side of the square is the early 19th-century neoclassical church of El Templete. Three paintings in the interior, by Jean-Baptiste Vermay, a pupil of Jacques Louis David, commemorate the city's earliest Catholic ceremonies, including the first Mass celebrated here in 1519.

Calle Obispo

One of the most colourful streets in La Habana Vieja, it boasts at No. 117 the town's oldest remaining house (1648), a single-storey building repainted bright blue and white with fine tiled roof. On the same side, the Hotel Ambos Mundos at the corner of Mercaderes, has preserved Ernest Hemingway's room as a small museum, with his bed, one of his old Royal typewriters and other memorabilia, including a facsimile of his manuscript of *For Whom the Bell Tolls*. There is a splendid view of the old town from the hotel's rooftop bar. Across the street is the popular Café Paris.

Continuing towards Parque Central, you pass several handsome old shops with fine carved wood counters, notably the 19th-century Farmacía Taquechel at No. 155. This was the heart of the old town's financial district, as witness the Corinthium columns of the Comité Estatal de Finanzas. Canada is still Cuba's privileged North American business partner, and the Bank of Nova Scotia has its monumental premises just a block north, on O'Reilly and Cuba.

Cathedral

Northwest of Plaza de Armas, the cathedral is the old city's proudest edifice (open only for the Sunday mass). With subtly differing towers flanking the gently concave baroque façade, it lends an Italianate, theatrical appearance to the square. The St Ignatius church of the Jesuits, not quite completed at the time of their expulsion in 1767, became the Catedral de San Cristóbal de La Habana 20 years later. Archbishop of Espada enlarged it in the 19th century, adding a marble floor and baroque altars with neoclassical mahogany. The frescoes behind the high altar are by Giuseppe Perovani, and the paintings of the *Ascension*, *Last Supper* and *Power of the Church* by Jean-Baptiste Vermay. The much disputed remains of Christopher Columbus were brought here from Santo Domingo and jealously held in the main chapel until begrudgingly transferred to Seville at the end of Spanish rule in 1898.

Plaza de la Catedral

A popular arts and crafts market is held on the cathedral square, particularly active at the weekend. Directly opposite the cathedral is the Museum of Colonial Art housed in the square's oldest building, Palacio de los Condes de Casa Bayona (1720). It exhibits furniture, porcelain and other Spanish colonial ornaments.

On the east side of the square is the Palacio del Marqués de Arcos (1746), which became the city's main post office in the 19th century and today houses an office of Telecorreo Internacional, with a carved stone mask still operating as a mailbox. Next to it stands the 18th-century Casa de Lombillo, now used as an education museum. Across the plaza, in the Casa del Marqués de Aguas Claras, a beautiful inside courtyard with a marble fountain now serves as the terrace of the El Patio bar and restaurant.

Next to the cathedral, at San Ignacio 22, is the Centro Wilfredo Lam. Along with shows of African, Asian and Latin American artists, the gallery exhibits the works of this Cuban painter, a leading Surrealist much influenced by his contact with Picasso and African folk art.

More Museums and Mansions

In the old town, you will come across many colonial mansions transformed into museums: the 17th-century Casa del Obispo, at Calle Oficios 8, was a priests'

Still roadworthy—and all set to take you on a tour of the city.

house, then a pawnshop and, with a certain sequential logic, now the Museo Numismático exhibiting coins and medals dating back to the beginnings of the Spanish colonial era.

At nearby Oficios 12, the 18th-century Colegio San Ambrosio displays Islamic art in the Casa del Árabe. The Museo del Automóvil at Oficios 13 exhibits vintage cars, a speciality of Havana since the "American" era of the 1930s, 40s and, particularly, the garish 50s.

At Calle Obrapía 158 is one of the town's more ornate baroque residences, early 17th-century and expanded in the 1780s. Di-

rectly opposite, Casa de África displays African artefacts and cult-objects of the Afro-Cuban *santería* religion.

On Mercaderes between Lamparilla and Obrapía, the Casa de Simón Bolívar is dedicated to the *Libertador* (1783–1830) of Peru, Columbia, Ecudaor, Bolivia and his native Venezuela. The house was recently renovated by Venezuela as a museum that gives an excellent idea of the classical Spanish colonial mansion—with verdant arcaded patios and marble staircase to the upper galleries tracing the life of the national hero. The nearby statue is a replica of his monument in Bogotá. 21

Cuba's grand Capitolio Nacional was built at the height of the depression.

At Obrapía No. 111, the Casa de Oswaldo Guayasamín is the Havana home of Ecuador's best-known artist. It is now a museum of his socially conscious paintings, including a Christ-like portrait of Fidel Castro, while offering a glimpse of one of the town's most elegant 18th-century houses.

Plaza Vieja

Created in the 16th century as a marketplace, principally for the Spanish slave trade, the square was originally known as Plaza Nueva after the army had expropriated Plaza de Armas. After a spell as a covered food market and car park, it is now being attractively restored with a handsome marble fountain and renovated façades on the old colonial buildings. The finest is the Casa del Conde de Suan Juan de Jaruco, on the corner of Calle Muralla and San Ignacio, with shops and galleries of the Cuban Arts and Crafts Foundation around the charming arcaded courtyard. it was built in 1670 and enlarged in the 18th century.

At the corner of Muralla and Inquisidor, the old Palacio Viena recalls its ornate Art nouveau beginnings of 1906.

The neoclassical Casa de las Hermanas Cárdenas (corner of Brazil and San Ignacio) was built in 1805 and became the home of the Philharmonic Society, now an art institute.

Two Writers' Shrines

Just off Plaza de la Catedral on Calle Empedrado is the Alejo Carpentier museum, assembling memorabilia of the great Cuban novelist in the house that is said to have inspired his historical novel, *El Siglo de las Luces* (Explosion in a Cathedral). Its better-known neighbour is the Bodeguita del Medio, a favourite bar of Hemingway and still the place to get one of his favourite drinks, the rum-laced *mojito*.

Churches

Since Fidel Castro's reconciliation with the Vatican, the city's churches have undergone a remarkable transformation. Here are the main attractions.

Nuestra Señora de Belén (1720), corner of Luz and Compostela, is a charming baroque church fronting what was Havana's first convent. The cluster of six cloisters passed from the Congregation of Bethlehem to the Jesuits in the 19th century before being taken over in 1925 by the Academy of Science. Its monumental 18th-century arch spanning Calle Acosta was the gateway to the old Jewish quarter.

Espíritu Santo, corner of Acosta and Cuba, was built by freed African slaves in 1638, with ancient catacombs in its crypt. The delicately carved wooden ceilings are fine examples of the Moorish influence on Spanish architecture. It is renowned as a sanctuary for fugitives from justice.

Nuestra Señora de la Merced (1755–1876), corner of Merced and Cuba, has a handsomely dec-

THE OTHER *MAXIMO LÍDER*

Havana jokers often remark that their city has two dictators, the second and no less powerful being Eusebio Leal, the city's official art historian (*Historiador de la Ciudad*). He is in charge of the wholesale reconstruction and renovation of the Spanish colonial mansions and other monuments in and around La Habana Vieja. He decides quite autocratically what can and cannot be renovated. Even though his people must often resort at best to *façadismo*—keeping the old façade but entirely rebuilding everything behind it, it is generally recognized that he is doing an efficient and tasteful job. Many of the mansions are being converted into hotels and elegant restaurants—under the management of the Habaguanex company of which Señor Leal is the chief executive officer.

orated interior, most notably the Esteban Chartrand frescoes on the ceiling.

San Francisco de Asís, on the south side of the busy Plaza de San Francisco, was built in 1591 and remodelled in its present baroque style in 1720. Its tall cubic belfry is a dominant feature of the Havana skyline. The church of Catholicism's least material of saints shares the square with the equally monumental old Stock Exchange (Lonja del Comercio).

City Centre

In the area west of Habana Vieja, the buildings and monuments of Centro Habana, almost all post-colonial, chart Havana's emergence as an independent republic.

Main Railway Station

The sprawling Estación Central de Ferrocarriles is a good place to start. It exhibits the locomotive, *La Junta*, that opened up the line between Havana and Matanzas in 1843 (the line south to the sugar plantations of Bejucal and Güines, inaugurated six years earlier, was the first railway in Latin America).

At the southeast corner of the railway yard, off Avenida de Bél-

gica, one of the few remaining stretches of the old city wall still stands.

José Marti Museum

Just east of the station, at Calle Leonor Pérez 314, is the modest blue and white house, birthplace of José Martí (1853–95). Now a museum to the father of Cuban independence, it exhibits the poet-journalist's manuscripts, letters and photographs.

Park of American Fraternity

At the southeast corner of the park, the 1837 Fuente de la India is a white marble fountain showing an Indian maiden riding high on four dolphins; it celebrates the Indies that Columbus thought he had discovered. The park itself was inaugurated in 1892, on the 400th anniversary of that discovery. Solemnly fenced in, the ceiba silk-cotton tree of American Fraternity was ceremoniously planted in 1928, in soil brought here from every country in the Americas.

Cigar Factory

Tucked away on the west side of the huge Capitol building is the Réal Fábrica de Tabacos Partagás, one of the country's most venerable Havana cigar factories, founded by Jaime Partagás in 1845. On the morning tours, Monday to Friday, you can watch

Cuban cigars, the world's best, are to be treated with respect.

25

IT'S ONLY MONEY

More than Fidel Castro, Che Guevara has remained the people's authentic revolutionary hero. They particularly appreciate his opposition to Cuba's subservience to the Soviet Union. For just six months in 1960, Che served as finance minister, until he realized he was not cut out for an office job. The national bank notes he was empowered to sign during that time have become a great collector's item. He signed them simply "Che".

the 400 workers rolling these still coveted symbols of capitalist prosperity.

The Capitol

Capitolio Nacional, the gigantic, more ornate version of Washington's Capitol, was built at the height of the economic depression (1929–32); it epitomizes the illusions of grandeur of the reformist-turned-dictator Gerardo Machado. Seat of the republic's Senate and Congress until the Revolution of 1959, it is now the home of Cuba's Academy of Sciences. Inside is one of the world's biggest indoor statues, a Jupiter in bronze, 17 m (55 ft) tall. Set in the paving beneath the dome—62 m (203 ft) high—is a (fake) 24-carat diamond marking the city's exact centre, the point from which all distances are measured.

Palacio de Aldama

Standing behind the Capitol on Avenida de Bolívar, this most imposing of the city's 19th-century neoclassical buildings was the opulent home of a Spanish financier. His family held subversive meetings there promoting Cuban independence and until it was confiscated by the Spanish colonial authorities.

With its grand Doric-columned portico, the mansion has a beautifully wrought iron doorway and balcony. Inside what is now the Historical Institute of the Cuban Workers' Movement, the friendly concierge may let you sneak a look at the grand monumental coloured marble interior.

Paseo de Martí

The long, broad avenues where Havana's 19th-century gentry would take their evening stroll were modelled on the *paseos* of Madrid and other major Spanish cities. Indeed, the Paseo de Martí was originally named after the Spanish capital's Prado. Today, that gentry has gone, but visitors can still take a leisurely *paseo* of their own alongside the parks, past the Capitol, theatre and grand hotels out to the sea shore of the Straits of Florida.

The Gran Teatro merits a close-up view, both inside and out.

Gran Teatro de La Habana

This astonishing neo-rococo pile dates back in part to the first half of the 19th century. Sarah Bernhardt and Enrico Caruso both appeared here. Even if you cannot get tickets for performances of the much admired Cuban ballet and opera companies, it is worth taking a look at the auditorium, almost as extravagant as the exterior.

Two Grand Hotels

Just along Paseo de Martí, the Inglaterra hotel is a neoclassical monument in its own right. It was in the hotel's Louvre banquet hall that José Martí made his fiery speeches for Cuban independence in the 1870s, startling his audience at one point by breaking his sword. Across the Paseo in Parque Central is his marble statue (1905).

A couple of blocks north of the park is the equally splendid Hotel Sevilla (1908), favoured by Enrico Caruso. This is where the rum and pineapple cocktail called a "Mary Pickford" was first invented.

Palacio de Bellas Artes

The National Fine Arts Museum has some interesting European and Cuban paintings in collections from the 16th century to the 27 present day. The strength of the Cuban national spirit seems to infuse life into even the most obviously "political" paintings of the Revolution.

In a pavilion immediately in front of the museum is the most hallowed relic of that Revolution, the *Granma* motor launch in which Fidel Castro and his guerrilla army sailed to Cuba in 1956. Access to the pavilion is via the Museo de la Revolución.

Museo de la Revolución

With his often wry sense of history, Fidel Castro chose Batista's opulent presidential palace—entrance at Refugio 1—as the appropriate place in which to document the history of the Cuban Revolution. Of the island's many museums devoted to the heroic events, this is the most vivid and complete.

In front of the museum rests the tank in which Castro patrolled the battlefield at the Bay of Pigs in 1961.

More Cigars

Across the road from the museum is Real Fábrica de Tabacos La Corona, the tobacco factory that created the Cohiba, Castro's favourite cigar—until he was forced to give them up. Take a morning tour to see it being hand-rolled, along with the Romeo y Julieta and Montecristo.

Malecón

Built as a 20th-century counterpart to the old Spanish colonial *paseos*, this promenade linking Centro Habana to Vedado curves gracefully along the seafront with gaily painted façades in pastel blues, pinks, yellows and greens creating a new landmark for the city. The eastern starting point is the Castillo de San Salvador de la Punta, a 16th-century fortress at the tip of the channel leading into the harbour. Malecón continues 8 km (5 miles) west to the old tower of La Chorrera at the mouth of the Almendares river. The atmosphere is less solemnly genteel than on the old *paseos* as young couples emerge from the Parque de los Enamorados (Lovers' Park) to take the air on the sea wall, sing and play guitars. Older folk come here to fish, play cards or dominoes. Monuments on the way to Vedado include the 24-storey National Hospital, a statue to 1895 war-hero General Antonio Maceo and the 18th-century Spanish San Lázaro watchtower.

Vedado

West of Centro Habana, the commercial and hotel district of Vedado is the former bastion of US entrepreneurs, high and low. They established their offices and banks here after the military occupation of 1898 and, as tour-

The setting sun enhances the timeworn façades of the Malecón.

ism developed in the 30s, added Las Vegas-style hotels, casinos, nightclubs and restaurants.

The more shady establishments reached their peak under Fulgencio Batista in the 50s and disappeared along with him in January 1959.

Vedado's American-style grid system of streets is still numbered (odd numbers north-south from Malecón, Calle 1, 3, 5, and even numbers west-east, Calle 2, 4, 6) or lettered (Calle A, B, C).

On the northern edge of Vedado across the Malecón, the 1926 Monumento a las Victimas del *Maine* commemorates the 266 US sailors killed in a mys-

terious explosion that destroyed the ship in Havana harbour in February 1898. The Americans blamed a Spanish mine, the Spanish suspected an ammunition accident on the ship, while Cuban Revolutionaries, in an inscription added to the monument, accuse American agents of creating the incident as a pretext for subsequent US intervention.

Hotel Nacional

Having too gracefully aged, even by Cuban standards, since its 1930s heyday, this elegant hotel (corner of Calles 21 and O) was splendidly rebuilt in the early 1990s, evoking Havana's old 29 sparkle. It had its moment of turbulence in 1933 when Fulgencio Batista burst in with troops to capture—and summarily execute—Cuban Army officers seeking refuge here during the "Sergeants' Coup".

Today, the lobby and bar offer a nostalgic echo of calmer days that saw Winston Churchill, Frank Sinatra and Ava Gardner among its guests.

La Rampa

Officially Calle 23, the Vedado's main street is the centre of its night life, off-beat bars, cabarets and nightclubs. On La Rampa by day you can see the avant-garde architecture of Pabellón Cuba and the town's largest hotel, Habana Libre, formerly the Hilton "liberated" by Castro for his first HQ in January 1959.

Opposite, long queues indicate the entry to the Coppelia ice-cream park, featured in Tomás Gutiérrez Alea's film *Strawberry and Chocolate* and a favourite meeting point, despite the erratic opening hours.

Universidad de La Habana

What was founded in 1728 as a Dominican seminary became a secular university in the 19th century. The vast neoclassical complex now hosts 30,000 students. Opposite the monumental stairs of its main entrance, the memor-

ial to Julio Antonio Mella pays tribute to a student leader assassinated by the dictator Machado in 1929. Beyond the gateway, inside the campus on Plaza Ignacio Agramonte, are two museums: Natural Sciences, devoted to the island's flora and fauna; Anthropology, containing Cuba's best collection of pre-Columbian art.

Museo Napoleonico

Just east of the University on Calle San Miguel, corner of Ronda, is one of Havana's most curious museums. In an Italian-style palazzo, wealthy Cuban businessman Julio Lobo has installed a formidable museum on four floors dedicated to his hero, Napoleon Bonaparte and the French Revolution. His collection of fascinating authentic memorabilia from all around the world includes paintings and sculptures of the Emperor, but also of Wellington, his nemesis at Waterloo. Among the quasi-religious relics are a piece of Napoleon's coffin and some of his hair. You can also see the last letter of Louis XVI and a note scribbled by his wife Marie Antoinette.

Escalona Murals

Further east, on a wall of the little pedestrian street Callejón de Hamel between Hospital and Arambura, are the unique paintings of Salvador Escalona, a sage of the Afro-Cuban cult of *santería*. Influenced by the Spanish masters Picasso, Dalí and Miró, this self-taught artist renowned throughout Latin America has produced a bizarre series of inspirational friezes in a style of naïve surrealism. His mystical easel-works and sculptures are on sale in a nearby gallery.

Plaza de la Revolución

South of Vedado, this most celebrated of Havana squares is vast enough to be considered a neighbourhood all to itself. It can contain—and for the great political rallies at the height of Fidel Castro's popularity in the 1960s, it did hold—up to a million spectators. Mass demonstrations take place here on May 1 and the Revolution's anniversary, July 26. But the gigantic proportions were conceived by Gerardo Machado, as a companion piece to his huge Capitolio Nacional, and most of the buildings were the work of Batista.

Castro made his greatest speeches from a podium at the star-shaped Memorial José Martí rising 142 m (465 ft) behind his seated marble statue. Though there are no statues or images of Castro himself, Che Guevara is portrayed in a mural on the Ministry of the Interior, with his slogan *Hasta la Victoria Siempre* ("To Victory, Always").

Necrópolis Cristóbal Colón

West of the Plaza de la Revolución is the monumental cemetery in which are buried the nation's military and political heroes—General Máximo Gómez, reformist Eduardo Chibás, who committed suicide in protest against government corruption in 1951, and veterans of the 1959 Cuban Revolution in a separate Pantheon.

City Outskirts

Sightseeing away from the city centre takes you out to the two old fortresses across the harbour channel, Ernest Hemingway's home at San Francisco de Paula, the splendid greenery of Parque Lenin, and the eastern resort beaches, Playas del Este. Cuba's most celebrated nightclub and floorshow, the Tropicana, is west of the city centre at Marianao.

El Morro

Castillo de los Tres Santos Reyes Magnos del Morro—"El Morro" for short—was built in 1589. In the 16th and 17th centuries, a chain 250 m (820 ft) long was linked up each night to the fortress of La Punta to block shipping in the harbour channel. Well-nigh impregnable to attack from the Florida Straits, El Morro was captured in 1762 by the British, who tunnelled under the ramparts from the landward side. 31

The Playas del Este are just a short ride from Havana's centre.

The castle now houses a small maritime museum. The lighthouse was erected in 1845.

Fortaleza de San Carlos

Less crowded than El Morro but just as interesting is the bigger Fortaleza de San Carlos de la Cabaña, built in 1763 to correct the deficiencies exposed by the British invasion. In the 20th century, the massive fortress served Cuban dictators Machado and Batista as a military prison. Che Guevara made it his headquarters and it now serves as an army museum—Museo de Fortificaciones y Armas—displaying mainly weapons. Dating back to Spanish colonial times, a cannon-firing ceremony in 19th-century uniform begins each evening at 8.30 p.m.

Hemingway's Home

At San Francisco de Paula, 15 km (9 miles) southeast of the city centre, is Finca la Vigía where Ernest Hemingway lived on his prolonged stays in Cuba from 1939 to 1960, a year before he committed suicide in Idaho. The villa has been transformed into a Hemingway museum and retains his memorabilia and furniture, including the desk at which he *stood* to write his six hours each morning.

Parque Lenin

Some 20 km (12 miles) south of town, the park covers 670 ha (1,655 acres) of beautiful greenery, with formidable old tropical trees around the Embalse Pase Sequito lake. South of the lake stands a bronze monument to the late Celia Sánchez who was instrumental in having the park built. Lenin is duly honoured with a white marble monument up on a hill a little further south.

Across the highway near ExpoCuba railway station, the National Botanical Gardens are worth a visit, particularly for their Japanese garden.

National Aquarium

On Avenida 1ra at the corner of Calle 60 in the western suburb of Miramar, the seafront Acuario Nacional has re-opened to display exotic tropical and sub-tropical fish of the Caribbean and from further afield.

Scale Model of Havana

Also in Miramar just south of Avenida 1ra on Calle 28, a large-scale model of Havana gives an excellent idea of the city's historic development and recent expansion.

Cojímar

Just east of Havana, one of the most attractive of the mushrooming Hemingway "shrines" is this little fishing village where the writer set his novel *The Old Man and the Sea* in 1952. Basing its hero on Cojímar pal Gregorio Fuentes, the story, which greatly contributed to Hemingway's Nobel Prize for Literature two years later, tells of an old fisherman who captures a giant marlin after a titanic fight, only to see it snatched from his boat and gobbled up by sharks on the long voyage home.

On the town's jetty near the old Spanish fort (now occupied by the coast guard), the fishermen used parts of their old boats to construct a monument around a gilded bust of their illustrious friend. One of the writer's favourite restaurants, the seafront La Terraza, is decorated with photos of fisherman Hemingway and his friend Fidel Castro.

Playas del Este

The pine-shaded sands of Havana's beaches stretch from Bacuranao and Mégano to Santa María del Mar and Guanabo. Beginning about 18 km (11 miles) east of the capital, they make an easy day trip from the city or an overnight stay to enjoy the water sports and deep-sea fishing. The largest concentration of hotels is at Santa María del Mar, which consequently has the most crowded beach. Guanabo is a favourite with the Cubans themselves.

THE NORTHWEST
Varadero, Cárdenas, Matanzas, Mariel,
San Diego de los Baños, Soroa, Viñales Valley,
Pinar del Río, Playa Bailen, Tobacco Country,
Playa María La Gorda

One in three visitors to Cuba heads straight for its biggest resort, Varadero. Many cannot tear themselves away from its magnificent beaches on the Atlantic Ocean. At the western end of the island, beyond Havana in the Pinar del Río province, enjoy the quieter, slower pace of rural Cuba in the pretty countryside hugging the Cordillera de Guaniguanico mountains. At Viñales, you can go horseback riding to admire the strange *mogote* mounds and explore the caves.

The Pinar del Río region is of course most famous for producing the tobacco that goes into the best Havana cigars. The main plantations are concentrated in the triangle formed by the towns of Pinar del Río itself, San Luis and San Juan y Martínez and, further west, in the fabled Vuelta Abajo area along the Cuyaguateje river.

But tobacco accounts only for a small fraction of the region's farmland. Fields of sugar cane blanket the eastern plains until rice paddies take over to fill the marshlands south of Los Palacios. Cattle herds graze the Guaniguanico foothills and citrus orchards, grapefruit and oranges, occupy the western area around Sandino.

Varadero

The hotels and beaches stretch along 20 km (12 miles) of white sands on the Hicacos peninsula jutting out from the Atlantic coast of Matanzas province. Cuban holiday-makers have been coming here since 1872, but it was launched as an international resort with the 1929 purchase of land here by US munitions and chemical magnate Eleuthère Irénée Du Pont. He built himself a huge sprawling mansion, yachting harbour, iguana farm, golf course and airstrip. At the height of the American Depression, other American millionaires followed, including Mafia boss Al Capone from Chicago—his home is now a restaurant named La Casa de Al.

Today, Canadian and European tourists come to Cuba's most popular playground for its

An intriguing backdrop of limestone mogotes in the fertile Viñales Valley.

super water sports facilities by day and the countless *discotecas* and the hotels' lavish cabaret floorshows by night.

Municipal Museum

On Calle 57, a mansion dating from the 1920s displays paintings from the Matanzas region and Indian artefacts. The upstairs balcony offers a splendid view over the Hicacos peninsula.

Parque Josone

For a little shady greenery away from the beaches, this landscaped park has neatly kept lawns around a pond, with a restaurant in the quaint Retiro Josone villa. At the eastern edge of the park is the Taller de Cerámica Artística (pottery workshop).

Du Pont Mansion

On Avenida Las Américas east of the town centre, you can get a look at the grand house that started it all by visiting the restaurant or the upstairs bar.

Delfinarium

About 5 km (3 miles) east of the Du Pont Mansion, watch the daily dolphin shows or, for an extra fee, dive in and swim with them yourself.

Cueva de Ambrosio

A series of 72 Indian wall-drawings was found in this cave in 1961. The geometrically patterned pictographs are similar to drawings found at Punta del Este on the Isla de la Juventud.

Cárdenas

For many visitors to Varadero, this 19th-century sugar planters' town is the first real taste of Cuban life away from the atmosphere of a modern resort, celebrated today as the home of Elián González. In streets laid out on a strict geometric gridplan, the houses with their stained-glass windows capture something of the old colonial elegance and horse-drawn carriages are still popular.

HIGHLIGHTS OF THE WEST

- **Varadero's Beaches**—white sands along Hicacos peninsula
- **Soroa's Orchid Garden**—400 species beside forest and waterfalls
- **Viñales Valley**—*mogote* mounds and caves with underground rivers
- **Pinar del Río**—cigar factory
- **Playa María La Gorda**—secluded beach for scuba diving

The town distinguished itself in the island's history as the first to hoist the Cuban national flag, in 1850, on Hotel La Dominica in Parque Colón. A tall flagpole at the seaward end of Avenida Céspedes commemorates the daring deed of General Narciso López. A year later the renegade was captured and executed.

Also in Parque Colón, in front of the cathedral, the town boasts one of the Americas' two oldest statues of Christopher Columbus, inaugurated in 1862, like the one in Havana's Palacio de los Capitanes Generales.

On the square of Parque Echevarría, the elegant neoclassical 19th-century city hall has been transformed into a municipal museum with a bizarre collection combining weapons, coins and medals with snails, seashells and butterflies.

The Fábrica de Ron Arrechabala near the port is the original plant for manufacturing Havana Club rum.

Matanzas

This important industrial port—petrochemicals, paper, textiles—has also long been a major cultural centre, known particularly for its music. The enigmatic name means "massacre" and may refer to an Indian uprising in 1509 when dozens of Spaniards were drowned in the bay. The city itself was founded at the end of the 17th century, benefiting

---

ADVANTAGES OF SMALL-TOWN FAME

The most famous little boy from Cuba was born in Cárdenas. Elián González was 6 years old when he made his momentous appearance on the world scene in November 1999. His refugee mother and her lover were drowned when their raft capsized off the coast of Florida. Elián survived and was taken to the Miami home of Cuban-American relatives. Themselves refugees from Cuba, they claimed custody of the boy until, on US Government orders, he was taken from their home on April 22, 2000, and returned to his father, Juan Miguel González. By then, Elián had become a political pawn in power and propaganda games between Havana and Washington and between President Bill Clinton and his adversaries in Congress. Ever since, the little boy's primary school has become a place of pilgrimage. The school and town have cashed in on the world spotlight with a fresh lick of paint for the benefit of foreign TV cameras. And after years on the waiting list, his teacher at last had a telephone installed to answer reporters' questions.

from the magnificent natural harbour. Its two rivers, the Yumurí to the north and San Juan to the south, provided transportation for the sugar planters, who set up their factories in the town. In the 19th century prosperity from this—and a boom in the slave-trade—attracted artists, musicians and writers, who produced the country's first newspaper. Freed slaves made the town a centre for their secret society for mutual aid, Abakuá. Musicians also shocked Spanish colonial high society with the creation here of the *danzón,* an Afro-Cuban version of courtly quadrilles in which couples *held* each other. It was the predecessor of the rumba, another Matanzas phenomenon.

Palacio del Junco

On Plaza de la Vigía, a charming square laid out between two bridges, the blue 19th-century planter's mansion with arcades on both street level and its upper storey now houses the Museo Histórico Provincial. It traces the region's story from pre-Columbian times to the present day, with exhibits devoted to slavery, the sugar industry, bourgeois culture and the Revolution.

Teatro Sauto

The neoclassical opera house was designed by Italian architect Daniele Delaglio. Enrico Caruso sang here, Sarah Bernhardt performed Alexandre Dumas' *La Dame aux Camélias,* and ballerina Anna Pavlova danced in 1915.

Museo Farmacéutico

In the centre of town on Parque Libertad, the superb 19th-century pharmacy of Frenchman Ernest Triolet is now a museum. It has preserved its handsome wooden counters and shelves, porcelain jars, Bohemian crystal phials, marble and bronze scales and a monumental table with multiple drawers that won a prize at the World's Fair of 1900.

Las Cuevas de Bellamar

Some 5 km (3 miles) southeast of Matanzas in the village of Alcancia, the grottoes have some impressive stalagmites and stalactites and cool natural pools. The one-hour guided tour takes you through a series of galleries stretching 2 km underground.

Mariel

A day-trip 45 km (28 miles) west of Havana to this town-behind-the-headlines has strictly curiosity value. The industrial port city became famous in 1980 as the embarkation point for the mass exodus of 125,000 Cuban *balseros* émigrés. Water sports enthusiasts appreciate the scuba-diving here.

San Diego de los Baños

Some 120 km (75 miles) west of Havana, this recently restored hot springs spa has been favoured by Cubans since the 18th century for the sulphurous waters' beneficial effect on respiratory and skin ailments. In keeping with the spa's old-fashioned ambience, enjoy the colonial charm of a drink on the terrace of the Hotel Mirador.

Soroa

At the heart of the Sierra del Rosario some 95 km (60 miles) from the capital, this cool and pleasant mountain resort has a superb forest and orchid garden nurtured by the region's heavy rainfall. The Orquidareo claims nearly 400 different species of orchids. The forest boasts two waterfalls, El Arco Iris and the spectacular El Salto, where you swim beneath the cascading waters. From the rocky Mirador or the Castillo de la Nubes, you can admire fine views over the whole park, recently declared a UNESCO-protected biosphere.

Viñales Valley

Some of Cuba's most alluring landscape is to be found in the valley—in fact, a cluster of valleys—lying serenely between the two ranges that make up the Guaniguanico, Sierra del Rosario to the east and Sierra de los Órganos to the west. The bizarre mound-like *mogotes*, overgrown limestone outcroppings, are scattered across the green valley floor like primeval bastions and ramparts covered by aeons of vegetation. Also around the village of Viñales, about 27 km (16 miles) north of the town of Pinar del Río, are caves eroded deep in the limestone bedrock by subterranean rivers.

Mogote Dos Hermanas

The Two Sisters mogote is notable for its Mural de la Prehistoria, 180 m (590 ft) long, painted on the rock face in 1961 by Leovigildo González, a disciple of Mexican artist Diego Rivera. The mural's primitive figures undergo perpetual renovation by painters lowered on ropes from the cliff top, a spectacular operation you can admire from a nearby restaurant over a plate of barbecued pork.

The Caves

Cueva del Indio was a refuge in the 16th century for Arawak Indians driven by the Spanish from their homes in the Camagüey plains. It was rediscovered in 1920, 6 km (4 miles) north of Viñales village. Explore its electrically lit interior on foot and then take a rowing boat on the underground river to a small waterfall at the other end—in all about 750 m (less than half a

39

mile). Closer to the village, Cueva de San Miguel has been converted into a bar—Disco-Bar Cuevas de Viñales.

Pinar del Río

The town was founded in 1774, following the settlement of rebel *vegueros*, tobacco-planters smuggling the best of their crop out to European connoisseurs to avoid paying duty to the Spanish government. The town soon established itself as capital of Cuba's tobacco industry. Its capture by General Antonio Maceo's troops in 1896 was a major factor in persuading the USA to intervene and stop Cuba becoming too independent. Today, linked to Havana by expressway, it is a pleasant combination of pink-tiled houses with neoclassical porticoes in the city centre and modern apartment buildings, schools and sports facilities on the outskirts.

Two Factories

Smaller than the major factories of Havana, the Fábrica de Toba-

---

THE FINE ART OF THE CUBAN CIGAR

Despite all the adverse publicity on health hazards, the cigar has held its own, along with champagne and caviar, as a symbol of the good life. The word comes from the Maya *zikar*, which in fact refers to the act of inhaling smoke, so as to induce in its users a state of clairvoyance. The Indian medicine men whom Christopher Columbus discovered on Cuba smoking the magic weed used a reed pipe, *tobago*. The tobacco plant was known as *cohiba*. It was the Spaniards themselves who developed the idea of rolling the leaves into cigars.

From seed to cigar-box is a roughly six-month process for the best cigars. Month-old tobacco seedlings are planted from late October to early December. In three months, they grow about 1.5 m (5 ft) high, with leaves 30 cm (12 inches) long and 25 cm (10 inches) wide. They are sheltered from the tropical sun by cheesecloth, and above that a roof of netting keeps out insects. Cedar trees bordering the plantations provide the wood for the cigar-boxes.

The hand-harvested leaves are hung to dry for one to two months in curing houses exposed to maximum sunlight. The best leaves are baled and shipped to factories in Havana, where they are briefly moistened and again dried out. Three sorts of tobacco go into the final cigar: filler tobacco in a binder leaf, held 30 minutes by a special press, and then hand-rolled in the all-important high-quality wrapper leaf.

cos Francisco Donatien is a good place to get a close-up view of the cigar-rolling process—with the possibility of buying the product (or at least the attractive cigar-boxes) in the adjacent shop.

Something to savour while puffing your cigar—or not—is the potent local guava brandy, Guayabita del Pinar, distilled sweet or dry at the Fábrica de Bebidas Casa Garay, which welcomes visitors to the plant for a free tasting.

Two Museums

The region's flora and fauna are exhibited in the Museo de Ciencias Naturales, housed in a startling early 20th-century *palacio* mixing Gothic, rococo and Egyptian pharaonic styles. The Museo Provincial de Historia relates the region's history from its first Indian habitants to the present day, with some good examples of Spanish colonial furniture, and the memorabilia of a much cherished local hero, Enrique Jorrín, creator of the chachachá.

Tobacco Country

The highway southwest of Pinar del Río, takes you through the two tobacco villages of San Luis and San Juan y Martínez. Here you will see the plantations in all their green splendour, often surrounded by graceful cedar trees that provide the wood for the

cigar boxes, and the tobacco curing houses *(vegas)* thatched with palm fronds.

Further west, centred on the town of Guane, is the cigar connoisseurs' paradise, Vuelta Abajo, blessed with a unique sandy soil and humid microclimate.

Playa Bailen

About 80 km (50 miles) south of Pinar del Río, this fine beach stretching out around the Bahía de Cortés is much more popular with Cuban families than tourists, especially at weekends. As a result, there are plenty of spontaneous beach-parties, good music. Bring your own bottle of rum and join in the fun.

Playa María La Gorda

Tucked into the Bahía de Corrientes, a bay of rugged cliffs that sheltered British and Portuguese pirates, this small resort has a fine beach for scuba-diving. The Maria of its name is said to have been the buxom Venezuelan sweetheart of sailors who stranded her here but frequently returned for visits.

Bird-watchers can be spotted in the nature reserve of the Guanahacabibes Peninsula, with its abundance of parakeets, partridges and, for the sharp-sighted, the *zunzuncito* bee-hummingbird, said to be the smallest bird in the world.

41

THE CENTRE

Cienfuegos, Santa Clara, Bay of Pigs, Trinidad,
Valle de los Ingenios, Sancti Spíritus, Camagüey

Cuba's heartland stretches from the sugar and coffee plantations around the Guamuhaya (or Escambray) mountains of Cienfuegos to the cattle pastures of the Camagüey plains. As the region that has traditionally separated the poor peasants of the Oriente from the wealthy land-owners around Havana in the west, it has played a significant role in Cuban history. It has witnessed the early Spanish settlers' fleeting dreams of gold in Trinidad, the first serious campaigns for independence led by the sugar-planters and Camagüey cattle barons, and, in modern times, Che Guevara's decisive defeat of Batista's troops at Santa Clara in 1958, followed three years later by the débâcle of the Cuban exiles' Bay of Pigs invasion. And the Ancón peninsula offers the best beaches on Cuba's south coast.

Cienfuegos

Settled in 1819 by French colonists from Louisiana (as a sequel to the US purchase of French territories from Napoleon), the city still has a certain Gallic flavour in the neoclassical façades of its long broad avenues—and in the blond hair and blue eyes of many of today's 125,000 residents. It is named after the Spanish governor who invited in the French settlers to create a "racial balance" with the Afro-Cubans in the area. It is the world's leading sugar port.

Parque José Martí

Guarded by two marble lions, the tree-shaded square with a statue of José Martí in the middle is bordered by many of the town's major buildings, all built in the late 19th century. The grand Teatro Tomás Terry was named in honour of a Venezuelan businessman. The auditorium, where both Enrico Caruso and Sarah Bernhardt performed, is worth a look for its mahogany seats and fanciful ceiling fresco. Opposite the theatre is the provincial government's imposing neoclassical Palacio del Gobierno.

The twin-towered cathedral, on the east side of the park, has French stained-glass windows. On the west side, the Benjamin Duarte cultural centre offers occasional concerts and a view from its *mirador* over Cienfuegos Bay.

The Prado

This is the citizens' preferred name for Calle 37, the *paseo* where they take their evening stroll. The broad avenue leads

In Trinidad, a town built on sugar, all roads lead to pretty Plaza Mayor.

south to the old aristocratic district of Punta Gorda. At the far end, the startling Palacio de Valle, a Moorish-Venetian folly built in 1917, is now a smart restaurant.

Castillo de Jagua

This 18th-century fortress was built at the mouth of Cienfuegos Bay to guard its narrow entrance against pirates. It is now a seafood restaurant. Easiest access is by boat from Marina Puertosol.

Jardín Botánico Soledad

Some 16 km (10 miles) east of town on the road to Trinidad, this pretty botanical garden is laid out over 90 ha (220 acres) near the Pepito Tey sugar mill. It boasts 300 varieties of palm tree, 65 varieties of fig and 200 cacti.

Santa Clara

The site of Che Guevara's grandest military exploit lies at the very centre of the island, some 60 km (38 miles) northeast of Cienfuegos. On Calle Independencia, the Monument to the Capture of the Armoured Train (*Monumento a la Toma del Tren Blindado*) commemorates the event together with a museum housed in five wagons of the train, alongside the guerrillas' bulldozer that derailed it. An enormous statue of Che in 43 military fatigues, rifle in hand, towers over the city's main square, Plaza de la Revolución, with an exhibition devoted to the legendary hero's life. His remains were brought from Bolivia to be buried in Santa Clara in October 1997. But the most imposing edifice in town, at the northwest edge of the Parque Vidal, is the 19th-century Teatro La Caridad, scene of a memorable performance by Enrico Caruso.

Bay of Pigs

A draw for history buffs—and scuba-divers—the site of the abortive invasion of US-trained Cuban exiles is an easy day trip from Cienfuegos—or across the island from Varadero. The landing took place on April 17, 1961 on Matanzas province's south coast at Playa Larga, a scruffy black beachhead at the north end of the marshy Bahía de Cochinos. On the east side of the bay at Playa Girón 35 km (21 miles) to the south, a museum documents with artefacts and photos what an accompanying 15-minute film calls "the first defeat of US imperialism in the Americas". Outside the museum is a Cuban Air Force plane used in bombing the supply ships. The nearby sheltered beach is more suited to swimming and snorkelling than to invasions.

Trinidad

With its cobbled streets and russet-tiled and Carrara marble-paved mansions, Cuba's third-oldest settlement, founded in 1514, is today an enchanting guardian of the Spanish colonial past. About 75 km (47 miles) east of Cienfuegos, the town was declared by UNESCO in 1988 a World Heritage Site—along with the sugar mills and slave quarters that made its fortune in the nearby Valle de los Ingenios.

Governor Diego Velázquez founded La Villa de la Santísima Trinidad in the belief that there were rich gold mines in an adjacent valley. To bless the undertakings of the colonists, Father Bartolomé de las Casas said Trinidad's first Mass, before becoming Apostle of the Indies

---

HIGHLIGHTS OF THE CENTRE

- **Trinidad**—Spanish colonial mansions around Plaza Mayor
- **Playa Ancón**—beach resort for swimmers, divers and bird-watchers
- **Valles de Los Ingenios**—relics of 19th-century sugar mills and slave watchtowers
- **Bay of Pigs**—historic site of exiles' 1961 aborted invasion

on his lone and fruitless anti-slave campaign. For his conquest of Mexico, Hernán Cortés recruited the town's fortune hunters disgruntled with gold-finds sifted in small quantities from surrounding river beds. Others stayed to breed cattle and plant more lucrative tobacco and sugar. Boom years in the mid-19th century enabled planters to build the grand houses that grace Trinidad today.

Plaza Mayor

With its lofty royal palm trees, the square presents a truly majestic setting for its aristocratic mansions and parish church, most of them in 18th-century neoclassical style and rebuilt in the 19th. The Iglesia Parroquial de la Santísima Trinidad dominates the northeast side of the square. The nearby Palacio Brunet, the splendid residence of a Spanish count, now houses the Museo Romántico displaying the sometimes over-opulent furnishings of the 19th-century sugar magnates.

On the northwest side of the square, the Archaeology Museum, devoted to Indian artefacts and natural history, is named after Alexander von Humboldt, the great German scientist-explorer who stayed here in 1801. On the southeast side, the Casa de Sánchez Iznaga has been linked to its 18th-century neighbour to contain the Museo de Arquitectura Trinitaria, presenting other typical interior décors of the town's rich planters. And in the Palacio Ortíz on the southwest side, local artists exhibit their works in what is now the Galería de Arte Universal.

The Side Streets

Much of the real charm of Trinidad is to be discovered in wandering away from the main square. South of Plaza Mayor on Calle Colón, there is a delightful open-air market of arts and crafts, with a small Fábrica de Tabacos nearby. Southwest at Plaza Santa Ana, a Spanish prison has been converted into a cultural centre for ceramics, sculpture and paintings, where you can also attend performances of the Trinidad Folk Ensemble.

On the northeast edge of town, at the end of Calle Simón Bolívar, you can get a bird's-eye view from the ruins of Trinidad's oldest church, 18th-century Ermita de la Popa.

Playa Ancón

This beach resort 12 km (7 miles) south of town makes a popular tourist base from which to visit Trinidad and nearby sights. Ancón, meaning a horse's hindleg, refers to the shape of a sailors' black rock landmark at Punta María Aguilar at the west end of the peninsula. The resort

45

has 4 km (2.5 miles) of beautiful white sandy beaches and a good offshore reef for scuba diving and snorkelling. Birdwatchers make for the tidal flats between Ancón and the fishing port of Casilda.

Valle de Los Ingenios

The picturesque valley beginning 8 km (5 miles) east of Trinidad is dotted with the ruins of sugar mills *(ingenios)*, manor houses, slave watchtowers, slave quarters and warehouses where Trinidad amassed its wealth in the 19th century. Most were destroyed by insurgent armies marching westwards in the wars of independence. A major landmark is the late 18th-century Manaca Iznaga sugar plantation 16 km (10 miles) east of Trinidad. Next to the manor house, the watchtower, 44 m (144 ft) high, from which the foremen looked for slaves and runaways is an eloquent monument to the huge fortune which Pedro Iznaga made from the slave trade rather than from sugar. His house is now a restaurant and bar.

Sancti Spíritus

For Spanish colonial atmosphere, the provincial capital on the Yayabo River offers an attractively sleepy version of Trinidad. The cobbled streets have been nicely restored, and its proudest monument is the handsomely frescoed parish church. The Iglesia Parroquial Mayor del Espíritu Santo, built in 1522, sacked and burned by pirates and rebuilt in 1680, is the oldest church in the country. It was here that Father Bartolomé de Las Casas preached his first anti-slavery sermon.

The Museo de Arte Colonial is housed in the *palacio* of 19th-century slave-owner Iznaga.

Camagüey

At the heart of the island's cattle country, the town has retained much of its colonial charm in the 18th-century mansions around Plaza San Juan de Dios, west of the Hatibonico river. The graceful cloistered hospital there is being transformed into a luxury hotel.

Unlike the grid plan of other Cuban towns, the old centre of Camagüey was deliberately built on an irregular pattern, intended to confuse attackers. As plundering English pirate Henry Morgan showed in 1668 and his French counterpart François Gramont 11 years later, the ruse didn't work very well. But the town recovered and built some fine edifices, notably the 18th-century cathedral with its Moorish roof, on Parque Ignacio Agramonte. The monumental Teatro Principal, on Padre Valencia, is important nowadays for the performances of Camagüey's much admired ballet company.

THE EAST

Santiago de Cuba, Gran Piedra, El Cobre, Bayamo, Holguín, Sierra Maestra, Guantánamo, Baracoa, Banes, Guardalavaca, Pinares del Mayarí

The eastern end of the island, traditionally known as Oriente, is now divided into five provinces: Guantánamo, Santiago de Cuba, Granma, Holguín and Las Tunas. Oriente is where Cuba's colonization by the Spanish began. Columbus landed somewhere near Guardalavaca, now second only to Varadero as the island's most popular beach resort. Baracoa and Bayamo were the first towns to be settled, and Santiago de Cuba was the country's first real capital, before Havana, and is still its greatest cultural rival. The region has always been a hotbed of rebellion. This was where the Afro-Cuban slaves staged their fiercest revolts, where the wars of independence started, where Fidel Castro led the Revolution from the mountains of the Sierra Maestra.

Oriente's natural beauties include the splendid wilderness of the Sierra Maestra national park, culminating in the island's tallest peak, Pico Turquino, and, further east, the forests around the Cordillera de la Gran Piedra. Cuba's longest river, Río Cauto, rises north of Santiago de Cuba to wind its way west into the Gulf of Guacanayabo.

Santiago de Cuba

In the lovely natural setting of its sheltered harbour, Cuba's second city (population 440,100) can trace the country's colourful history in its monuments and reflect the diversity of its peoples by a vibrant modern cultural life. For centuries, Santiago de Cuba's chief source of revenue came from its activity as Cuba's main trading port for African slaves. Afro-Cubans and mulattos are still in greater evidence here than in any other major Cuban town. Added to this, the mixture of American-Indian, French, Spanish and Chinese influences accounts for the often remarkable physical beauty of its men and women. And, as performed by such groups as the Ballet Folklórico Cutumba, the diversity of music and dance Afro-Cuban and otherwise—*guancó*, *tajona*, *conga oriental* and, imported by French refugees from Haiti, the *tumba francesa*. Only architecturally does the dominant influence remain Spanish colonial.

A day in the life of hilly Santiago, Cuba's vibrant second city.

49

Santiago de Cuba has always played a special role in Cuban history. The town was governor Diego Velázquez's choice as capital a year after its foundation in 1514. Hernán Cortés, Conquistador of Mexico, began his career as the city's first mayor. In modern times, it was the city that launched Cuba on the roads to independence and revolution. General Antonio Maceo, who fought in both 19th-century wars of independence, was born in Santiago de Cuba. Fidel Castro's first attack on Batista's forces on July 26, 1953 was launched against the city's Moncada Barracks. Thereafter, citizens gave his movement open and clandestine support during the guerrilla struggle and it was here, on New Year's Day, 1959, that Castro came to make his first public statement on the success of the revolution. Like Leningrad in the Soviet Union, Santiago de Cuba has been dubbed the nation's Heroic City.

Parque Céspedes

The square pays homage, with a bronze bust, to Carlos Manuel de Céspedes, the leader of Cuba's first war for independence in 1868. It remains the city's historic centre. At the northwest corner, the Casa de Diego Velázquez is the home of Cuba's first governor. Completed in 1522, it is the oldest house in the country. The businessman-politician liked to reside right over his money. His living quarters were upstairs, above the ground-floor trading house and gold foundry. Today, the Museo de Ambiente Histórico Cubano (Museum of the Cuban Historic Environment) displays domestic interiors of Spanish colonial homes from that of Velázquez to 19th-century slave-owners' dwellings.

At the other end of the historical spectrum, the balcony of the neoclassical Ayuntamiento (town hall) on the north side of the square was the stage chosen by Fidel Castro for his victory proclamation on the night of January 1, 1959.

On the south side of the Parque, the Catedral de Nuestra Señora de la Asunción stands on the site where the town's first cathedral was built in 1520. The victim of earthquake, fire and civil war, this 20th-century edifice is the fifth to be erected here, and is believed to conceal in its foundations the tomb of Diego Velázquez. The church treasury has some cherished manuscripts from the city's earliest days.

Calle Heredia

The street is named after José María de Heredia (1803–39), the Romantic poet whose birthplace at No. 260 is now a museum. The revolutionary ideas of this lyric champion of the American landscape forced him into exile in Mexico. His cousin, José María de Heredia y Giralt (1842–1905), went off to France to win fame as a sonneteer of the Parnassian school. Besides the amusing Museo del Carnaval at No. 303, the street has many cultural associations from the 19th century— the home of composer Rafael Salcedo at No. 208, of educator Juan Bautista Sagaria at No. 262 and of painters José Joaquín and Felix Tejada Revilla at No. 304.

The brothers' paintings can be seen in the neoclassical Museo Bacardí, on Pío Rosado, a side street running north from Heredia. Rum manufacturer Emilio Bacardí founded the museum in 1899. It is devoted to life, civilian and military, during the 19th-century campaigns for independence.

When visiting Calle Heredia, drop in at the Casa de la Trova at No. 208, where local musicians perform for their own enjoyment and that of the audience.

Moncada Barracks
The city's honoured place in the Cuban Revolution is celebrated most notably at what has been transformed into a school, with a section set aside as a museum to tell the story of Cuba from Spanish colonialization to the Revolution. It commemorates in particu-lar the unsuccessful assault on the Cuban Army barracks in July 26, 1953 mounted by Fidel Castro with his 100-strong rebel army. The assailants' bullet and shell marks on the building's façade were erased by Batista but "reinstated" by his successors.

San Juan Hill
In a park east of the city centre, American history buffs can visit the scene of the decisive battle in the 1898 Spanish-American War, when Theodore Roosevelt's Rough Riders made their famous charge up the hill against overwhelming odds. Surrounding the site are cannons, trenches and a bronze statue of the symbolic Rough Rider.

Bacardí Rum Factory
On the north side of town, factory tours—with a bar—are available to taste the brands that succeeded the original Bacardí company when it moved to Puerto Rico after the Revolution.

Gran Piedra
In the eastern portion of the Sierra Maestra range, the mountain, 1,214 m (3,983 ft) high, takes its name from a massive granite rock at the top, from which you can, on the proverbial clear day, see Jamaica and Haiti. A popular excursion 16 km (10 miles) southeast of Santiago de Cuba takes 51

The Virgin of Charity in El Cobre's basilica is the island's national saint.

you past a sculpture garden (Prado de las Esculturas) featuring artists from ten different countries and, closer to the top, a Botanical Garden with some fine orchids. The Gran Piedra itself is 25 m (82 ft) high and 51 m (167 ft) long and estimated to weigh over 63,000 tons. On the other side of the mountain is the Cafetal La Isabelica, a disused coffee plantation (transformed into a museum). It was set up by French refugees from Haiti at the beginning of the 19th century.

El Cobre

The revival of Catholic activities on the island has increased interest in Cuba's most revered pilgrimage church, the Basílica de Nuestra Señora de la Caridad del Cobre. It was off the coast here in the early 1600s that three Indian and Afro-Cuban fishermen "caught" a wooden statue of the Virgin Mary and Jesus floating in the bay. It became the object of a cult for Catholics as the Virgin of Charity and for Afro-Cuban followers of the *santería* religion as Ochún, Yoruba goddess of love. The present basilica was built in 1927, eleven years after Pope Benedict XV pronounced the statue to be the island's national saint. The offerings brought to honour the saint, on display at the

52

church visitor's centre, include a gold figurine of a guerrilla warrior left here by Señora Lina Ruz to protect her son, Fidel Castro, while he was fighting Batista in the Sierra Maestra. (Ernest Hemingway's Nobel Prize medal was also displayed here, but is now hidden away since being recovered from a thief in 1954.)

As its Spanish name suggests, the town is the centre of Cuba's copper mining industry—it has been ever since 1530—and you can see the present mine on a hill across from the church.

Bayamo

North of the Sierra Maestra mountains is the easy-going capital of Granma province, named in 1975 after the motor vessel that brought Castro and his followers to its coast in 1956. It was the second Spanish settlement to be founded (1513) by Diego Velázquez and made its fortune in colonial times as a centre for cattle-breeding and sugar. Its insurgents played a distinguished role in the wars for independence and, during Castro's 1953 attack on Moncada Barracks, launched a back-up assault on Batista forces.

Parque Céspedes is the centre of town, a pleasant tree-shaded square graced by the independence hero's bronze statue and surrounded by marble benches. Also in the park is a marble bust of Perucho Figueredo, composer of the national anthem. On the north side of the square is the Ayuntamiento (town hall) where Céspedes proclaimed Cuba's (short-lived) independence. His birthplace is at Calle Maceo 57 on the west side of the square and next door, the Museo Provincial tells Bayamo's illustrious history.

BAYAMO'S ANTHEM

The town's patriotic credentials are impeccable. Independence leader Carlos Manuel de Céspedes, born in Bayamo, commanded the rebel force that seized the town—for a couple of months—in 1868. That same year the citizens' exploits were celebrated in a song, *La Bayamesa*, that is still the national anthem:

"Al combate corred, Bayameses, que la Patria os contempla orgullosa.
No temáis una muerte gloriosa, que morir por la patria es vivir."
"Hurry to battle, Bayameses, for our country looks to you with pride.
Fear not a death in glory, for to die for your country is to live."

South of the centre on Calle Jose Martí, Torre de San Juan Evangelista is a unique monument from Bayamo's early days. The tower is all that remains of a 16th-century church destroyed in 1869 when the *Bayameses* burned the town down rather than leave it in the hands of the Spanish army.

Holguín

This lively town remains the centre of Cuba's sugar industry. It is reputed for its many tree-shaded squares, the most important being Parque de Las Flores, with its 18th-century San Isidoro church, and Parque Calixto García honouring with an equestrian statue the hero who liberated the town from the Spanish in 1872. The local Casa de la Trova on the corner of Parque Calixto García and Calle Maceo is a delightful place to hear—and dance to—the local Oriente music.

Sierra Maestra

This historic region is strictly for lovers of the great outdoors. It was hard for Batista's troops to get up into the Sierra Maestra mountains to smoke out the *Fidelistas* in the 1950s and it's not much easier now to enter Cuba's most magnificent national park. But hikers, bird-watchers and climbers insist that it's well worth the journey from Man-

zanillo's Sierra Maestra Airport via Yara. They enlist a guide at Villa Santo Domingo before journeying the last 5 km (3 miles) to the park entrance at Alto del Naranjo, 950 m (3,116 ft), with a rewarding view over the plains.

Comandancia de la Plata

Beginners can take an unhurried one-hour ramble along a signposted trail to Castro's old command post, the field hospital and the site of the guerrillas' transmitter, Radio Rebelde.

Pico Turquino

The trail around Cuba's highest mountain, 1,972 m (6,470 ft), leads you through the lush vegetation of virgin rain forest. This can be a one-day hike looping around back to Alto del Naranjo or a more challenging three-day guided mountain-trek (including the Turquino summit) with overnight camping and ending at Las Cuevas on the Caribbean coast.

Guantánamo

The US naval base, leased since 1903 and not due to be returned to Cuban sovereignty till 2033, is 21 km (13 miles) south of Guantánamo city, noisy and unprepossessing. The only view you may get of the base—mostly watchtowers, security fences, military airstrips and radar posts—is if you take a cruise yacht past Punta

Barlovento through Guantánamo Bay to the ports of Caimanera or Boquerón. Beyond the fences, trenches and minefields is a very comfortable garrison for 7,000 troops and relatives, with golf course, sports stadium, supermarkets and cinemas. In recent years the comfort has been disturbed by thousands of Cuban and Haitian refugees for whom Guantánamo serves as a transit station while they seek entry to the USA—and more often are sent back home.

Baracoa

On the north coast of Guantánamo province, the first town to be settled by the Spanish (1512) has great, if quiet, charm, especially along its seafront promenade, the Malecón, with the flat-topped El Yunque ("anvil") mountain in the background. In the Catedral de Nuestra Señora de la Asunción is the cross, *Cruz de La Parra*, that Columbus is said to have erected on landing near here. The Indian chief Hatuey,

executed by the Spanish in the year the town was founded, is portrayed in a bronze bust in front of the church. In the 18th century, the town built three forts against pirates. Fuerte Matachín houses the city's history museum, Fuerte de la Punta has a restaurant and El Castillo de Seboruco, a hotel.

Guardalavaca

With dazzling white sands, this beach resort is second in popularity only to Varadero. From Villa Don Lino to Estero Ciego and Bahía de Naranjo, the sailing, deep-sea fishing, wind-surfing, canoeing, scuba diving and snorkelling, as well as volleyball and tennis, are all first-class.

It was just west of Villa Don Lino, somewhere on Bariay Bay, that Columbus is believed to have made his first landing in Cuba, on October 28, 1492.

On Naranjo Bay, a boat-cruise takes you out to the island aquarium where dolphins and sea lions perform daily and you can swim

---

HIGHLIGHTS OF THE EAST

- **Santiago de Cuba**—Cuba's oldest colonial monuments on Parque Céspedes
- **Sierra Maestra**—spectacular hiking around Castro's guerrilla HQ
- **Guardalavaca**—superb beach resorts near Columbus' landing place
- **Baracoa**—quiet appeal of first Spanish settlement

All smiles in the tranquil town of Baracoa.

with the dolphins for an additional charge.

The remains of a hilltop Indian village have been excavated and preserved as a museum at Chorro de Maita, 8 km (5 miles) south of Guardalavaca.

Banes

Just over 30 km (19 miles) southeast of Guardalavaca, the little old town has a faded charm all its own but owes its importance to a museum boasting the island's largest archaeological collection of pre-Columbian artifacts. At Calle General Barrero 305, the Indo-Cuban Museum displays Arawak weapons, tools, jewels and pottery and the famous "Idol of Taïnos", a solid gold figurine dating back to the 13th century. In contrast, Banes can also claim on its streets one of the island's best collections of vintage Chevrolets, Cadillacs and Chryslers.

Pinares del Mayarí

Due south of Guardalavaca, pleasant mountain chalet accommodation has been built up on the high plateau cattle pastures of Altiplanicie de Nipe, alt. 600 m (1,968 ft). Ecotourism is gradually being developed here, and it's a perfect destination for hikes through the pine forests as a change of pace from the beaches.

ISLA DE LA JUVENTUD AND LOS CAYOS

Isla de la Juventud, Cayo Largo, Cayo Coco,
Cayo Guillermo, Cayo Romano

Cuba's offshore isles, islets, *cayos* (keys), and rocky sandbars with a tree or two, number in all 4,195, grouped in five archipelagos around the main island. The biggest, Isla de la Juventud, has been inhabited since prehistoric times, the others worth a visit have been partly transformed into modern beach resorts—Cayo Guillermo, Cayo Largo, Cayo Romano and Cayo Coco—each with superb white sands and good facilities for swimming, sailing and deep-sea fishing.

Isla de la Juventud

Part of the Canarreos archipelago, the island lies at the southern mouth of the Golfo de Batabanó, 100 km (60 miles) from the mainland and a 40-minute flight from Havana. Covering an area of 3020 sq km (1,165 sq miles), it has variously been a refuge for Siboney Indians, who left some of the finest cave-paintings in the Caribbean, hideout for pirates and penitentiary for political prisoners. It derives its modern name, Island of Youth, from Castro's ambitious programme in the 60s and 70s to bring thousands of young Cubans—and foreigners —to study and work the citrus plantations. Columbus called it El Evangelista. For Scottish novelist Robert Louis Stevenson, inspired by stories of Francis Drake, John Hawkins and Henry Morgan who moored their pirate ships along the west coast, it became Treasure Island. The Spanish colonists knew it as Isla de Pinos (Isle of Pines). Both José Martí and Fidel Castro were imprisoned here.

Today, it is gaining favour as an off-beat destination for scuba divers and nature lovers who appreciate the unspoilt wildlife— parakeets, pelicans and turtles on the coast, iguanas and crocodiles in the inland swamps.

Nueva Gerona

The island's capital lies on the Las Casas river between two small mountain ranges, Sierra de Caballos to the east and Sierra de Las Casas to the west. In the lively city centre, the Museo Municipal tells the island's story. Nuestra Señora de los Dolores, rebuilt in 1929 after a devastating hurricane, became famous in the 1950s as the church of Father Guillermo Sardiñas, the only Catholic priest to join Castro's guerrillas. The Museo de Historia Natural is devoted to the flora and fauna of the island and its archae-

You can have a beach all to yourself in the Cayos.

ology, notably reproducing the Siboney Indians' cave paintings from Punta del Este.

Two Prisons

Just 3 km (2 miles) southwest of town, beautifully situated at the foot of the marble and granite mountains of Sierra de Las Casas, is Finca El Abra, a hacienda in which José Martí was held under house arrest in 1870. A lot less charming, Presidio Modelo, 4 km (2.5 miles) east of Nueva Gerona, is modelled on the American maximum security prison in Joliet, Illinois. One of the four circular cell-blocks, completed in 1931, was host to Fidel Castro and his fellow assailant of the Moncada Barracks in 1953. It is now a museum celebrating the fact, while the remainder of the prison stands empty.

Punta Del Este

Some 60 km (37 miles) southeast of Nueva Gerona, four out of seven caves were decorated by Siboney Indians with splendid red and black wall-paintings. Archaeologists have counted 235 pictographs, the biggest being what is believed to be a solar calendar formed by 28 concentric red and black circles. An added bonus is a magnificent white sandy beach.

Punta Francés

On the Pirate Coast at the southwestern end of Siguanea Bay, this marine reserve is a popular spot for scuba diving among more than 50 caves with plenty of lobsters, turtles and other Caribbean creatures to join you.

Cayo Largo

This major beach resort 115 km (71 miles) east of the Isla de la Juventud is a favourite destination for scuba divers and birdwatchers. Cranes, pelicans, flamingos and bee-hummingbirds abound here along the flats.

The key boasts no less than 26 km (16 miles) of fine white sandy beaches. The most popular is the sheltered Playa Sirena facing west. A pleasant bicycle ride away to the east, Playa Blanca and Playa Los Cocos are less crowded, while Playa Tortuga, further out, attracts turtles to lay their eggs in the sand.

Cayo Coco

Covering an area of 364 sq km (140 sq miles), this is the best developed of the Camagüey archipelago's resort islands off the Atlantic coast. Causeways join it to the mainland across the Bay of Dogs, and to neighbouring Cayo Guillermo to the west and Cayo Romano to the east.

Cayo Coco boasts 21 km (13 miles) of impeccable white sandy beaches with first-class facilities for water sports. Flamingoes and pelicans strut along the coast, and the interior is covered by dense forest. Casasa on the northeast coast offers excellent opportunities for deep-sea fishing.

Cayo Guillermo

This little coral key of just 13 sq km (5 sq miles) was one of Ernest Hemingway's favourite fishing destinations and it is still good for marlin and mackerel, notably on boats chartered at the main hotel, Villa Cojímar (named after the village near Havana where Hemingway used to keep his boat).

Cayo Romano

The biggest isle of the archipelago, 926 sq km (357 sq miles), is popular with ramblers and nature lovers looking out for wild horses and zebu (wild oxen) roaming its unspoiled interior.

HIGHLIGHTS OF THE ISLES AND KEYS

- **Punta del Este**—Indian cave paintings on Isla de la Juventud
- **Punta Francés**—Juventud's best scuba diving on Pirate Coast
- **Cayo Coco**—spectacular luxury resort for water sports

CULTURAL NOTES

Arawak legacy. Indian culture was wiped out in Cuba by Spanish colonization, but some colourful words survived. *Barbacoa*, the Indians' wooden grill, was both bedstead and cooking grill, giving us "barbecue". Others include *canoa* (canoe), *hamaca* (hammock), *maíz* (maize or corn) and *patata* (potato), while *cikar* originally meant "inhaling smoke", not a cigar itself, and *tobago* was a smokers' reed pipe, only later tobacco.

Architecture. The elegant, even grand, colonial mansions still evident in Havana, Santiago de Cuba and Trinidad combine traditional elements of 16th- and 17th-century Spanish architecture and its earlier Moorish influences with the special needs of the Cuban climate. Notable Moorish features are the ornately carved wooden balconies, and the inner central patio around which the residential quarters are built. Entrances to 17th-century houses are relatively austere, with plain wooden doors set between simple Grecian-style pillars. The 18th-century mansions are more elaborately baroque. Entrances have monumental columns and sculpted pediments framing doors of carved wood-panelling.

They lead to a patio with ornate fountains, surrounded by porticoes on the ground floor and arcaded loggias on the upper storeys, to provide shelter from the sub-tropical sun and rains. The more sober neoclassical residences of the 19th century replace the upper-floor arcades with painted wooden window-shutters.

Béisbol. Yes, baseball is Cuba's national sport. A version of the United States' national game, which Arawak Indians called *batos*, existed here even before the Spanish arrived. It developed in its modern form with the growth of American influence in the late 19th century. Today every town has a baseball diamond. Encouraged by Fidel Castro who impressed Americans in 1950s with his talent as a pitcher, Cuba's national team is the best in Latin America and became Olympic champions at Atlanta, Georgia, in 1996.

Carnival. The Cubans' taste for festivities, public and private, reaches its climax with the two great carnivals celebrated in Santiago de Cuba, usually the last week in July, and in Havana for three weeks in August. For the capital's procession through the streets of La Habana Vieja, the neighbourhoods stage *comparsa*: spectacles of masked and costumed dancers, singers and musicians playing the conga. Each *comparsa* enacts a traditional theme. These include the life of the colonial aristocracy, *Los Marqueses*; the erotic or social satire of *Los Guaracheros*; or the legendary massacre of *El Alacrán* (the scorpion). Santiago's *comparsas* date back to the late 17th-century festivities for St James, the town's patron saint, but the music is resolutely modern Afro-Cuban. The distinctive "sound" of the Santiago carnival is provided by the *corneta China*, a flute introduced by Chinese immigrants in the 19th century.

Carpentier, Alejo. Cuba's best-known novelist (1904–80) was an acute observer of both the European and Cuban, particularly Afro-Cuban, scene. He spent several years in exile in pre-Castro years before directing a national publishing company and then serving as a Cuban diplomat in Paris. His first novel, *Ecué Yamba-O* (1933), gives a wonderful insight into the African roots of much of Cuban culture, while the short *Baroque Concerto* brings together the worlds of Europe and Latin America.

Gutiérrez Alea, Tomás. An important achievement of the revolution was the creation of the film industry, and Tomás Gutiérrez Alea (1928–96), Cuba's most famous director, has had remarkable freedom to express sensitive and humorous observation of social life and free-thinking criticism of bureaucracy. His best known works are *Fresa y Chocolate* (1994) and *Guantanamera* (1995).

Lam, Wilfredo. A major modern painter (1902–82) of Chinese and Afro-Cuban origin, he produced a sharp, almost mystic form of Surrealist painting which he developed in contact with Picasso and other European avant-garde artists. His appreciation of African folk art, so important to Picasso, was rooted in the culture of his island.

Music. In 1997, Buena Vista Social Club exploded on the international scene with records and the documentary film of Wim Wenders. In their 70s and 80s, singers Compay Segundo and Ibrahim Ferrer and pianist Rubén González suddenly became world stars. They re-introduced Europeans and Americans to the magic of Afro-Cuban music.

The richness of Cuban music derives from its mixture of

African and Spanish rhythms and instruments. The first European music that African slaves encountered in Cuba was that of the Catholic church and of Spanish military brass bands. To this was added the fiery drum rhythms learned in Africa, mostly in the Congo and Nigeria. The music was further enriched in the 17th century with the introduction of the Spanish *zarzuela*, a popular musical play using folk songs for witty and satirical treatment of everyday life. Between acts of the musical melodramas, the old satirical *tornadilla* songs were given a frankly erotic twist by *guaracheros* who specialized in sexual innuendos. Occasionally, a touch of bucolic "innocence" was added by *guajira* peasant songs created by workers on the sugar and tobacco plantations.

Spanish colonial musicians such as 19th-century composer-pianist Ignacio Cervantes spiced up traditional *danzón* folk-dances with Afro-Cuban rhythms. The most famous was his *Habanera*. In the 20th century, Amadeo Roldan included instruments of African origin in his symphonic orchestra. By the 1930s, Ernesto Lecuona, whose talents had attracted the attention of composers Maurice Ravel and George Gershwin and pianist Arthur Rubinstein, introduced the world to Afro-Cuban jazz with his band, the Lecuona Cuban Boys.

To the Spanish lute and guitar, Afro-Cuban musicians added the three-stringed *tres* and a whole panoply of percussion instruments for the all-important rhythm section: *bongo, udu* and *conga* drums; the *marimbula,* a xylophone plucked rather than hammered; *claves,* a pair of cylindrical hardwood sticks tapped one on the other in the palm of the hand; *maracas* rattles and serrated *güiros* fashioned from hollow gourds.

The romantic *trova* ballad had its beginnings in Santiago de Cuba, usually sung as a duet of *trovadores*, with a melancholy homespun philosophy. Best known is *Guantanamera*. More properly *Guajira Guantamera* (Guantánamo Peasant-Girl), this most famous of all Cuban songs, composed in 1929 by Joseíto Fernández, later had text added from José Martí's 1891 *Versos Sencillos*. To help you sing along, here's the first verse:

> *Yo soy un hombre sincero*
> *de donde crece la palma,*
> *y antes de morirme quiero*
> *echar mis versos del alma.*

(I'm a sincere man from where the palm tree grows, and before I die, I wish to sing these verses from the heart.)
You already know the chorus.

At the origin of practically all contemporary Cuban dance music is the *son* created in the 1920s in the mountains of Oriente province and the streets of Santiago. Classically, the songs are an exchange, often improvised, between soloist and the musicians' choral back-up. Typical is Compay Segundo's *Chan Chan*, now rivalling *Guantanamera* in popularity in Cuban bars.

The *rumba,* born in the backstreet slums of Havana and Matanzas and popularized in New York in 1920s, had its beginnings in religious rituals of the *santería*, where tune was less important than strong rhythm. Since, for white American tastes, Cuban rumba was felt to be too erotic in its slow *yambú* form or frenzied *guagancó,* Cubans proposed the more sedate *mambo* and *cha-cha-cha* in the 40s and 50s. Today, purists scorn the ever-popular salsa as a hybrid combination of Cuba's lyrical *son* with American jazz and rock'n roll, forgetting the mixed African and Spanish origins of all Cuban music.

Religion. After 40 years of subservience to the Marxist demands of the Cuban Revolution, open religious observance is back in force on the island. But it is not the Catholic church that is the most popular. The dominant religion remains *santería*, created 500 years ago by African slaves, amalgamating Christianity with the animist cults of Yoruba tribes of West Africa and others from the Congo region. Today, there are more than 10,000 *babalao* conducting the rituals of *santería*, while the Catholic churches, progressively re-opened since the visit of Pope John Paul II in 1998, number less than 300 priests.

Forbidden to practise their traditional cults, Afro-Cubans sought to preserve their cultural heritage by paying lip-service to Catholic saints and various aspects of the Virgin Mary while identifying these with their own tribal deities, *orisha*. In rituals similar to Haitian voodoo and Brazilian *macumba* and *ubanda,* these prestigious deified ancestors are invoked—like the saints and Virgin Mary in the Catholic church—to deal with the daily problems of the *santeros*. There are perhaps some 40 Cuban *orisha* in all, associated with the spirits of nature, but only half are the object of regular worship.

To the *santeros,* St Francis of Assisi "fronts" for Orula, a revered deity of knowledge and divination who is consulted, for instance, by worshippers em- 63 barking on an important journey. Orula's wife, Ochún, is the sensual goddess of love and femininity, identified with the Virgin Mary of Charity, patron saint of Cuba, whose statue was found off the coast of El Cobre (Oriente) in 1605. Ochún is nonetheless also the mistress of, among others, Ogun, god of iron, mountains and wisdom, famous for his great anger and assimilated to St Peter. The warrior *orisha* Chango is St Barbara, Christian patron of artillery. Jesus is associated with Oddua, god of the dead and of ghosts and invoked to revive the dying. Another important manifestation of Mary, the Virgin of Merced, is regarded as Obatala, who reigns as the divinity of creation, working for peace and harmony. The "black" Virgin of La Regla is Yemayá, goddess of the sea and sailors.

Only the *babalao* are permitted to interpret and communicate the oracles and prophesies made when the deities are consulted. They conduct rituals involving plants, grasses, sea shells and parts of animals. They also officiate at elaborate seven-day ceremonies initiating *yabo* (novices) into the *santería*. Following the sacrifice of the deity's animal, the new adept comes under the protection of a particular *orisha*, is given the appropriate necklace, bracelets and sacred stones and dressed in ceremonial costume. Family and friends pay tribute and the *babalao* describes the behaviour expected of the *yabo* in the future. For the first year, the novice dresses entirely in white and keeps at home in a large bowl the symbols of the patron orisha and other major deities—fruit, flowers and sometimes animal bones and claws.

Also originating in Nigeria and dating back to the days of slavery, *Abakuá* is the name of a secret society which, unlike *santería*, observes a monotheistic cult and strict moral code. This benevolent all-male fraternity has always practised mutual help, which began with the purchase of freedom for fellow slaves and associated itself with the island's campaigns for independence, the lodges of Free Masonry and, more recently, the Revolution led by Fidel Castro. *Abakuá* traces its foundation back to the myth of a princess who accidentally caught in her calabash the sacred fish *Tanze*, mouthpiece of the supreme deity, *Abasí*. The princess was sacrificed and her skin transformed into the sacred drum, *Ekwe*, which ever since has proclaimed in a secret chamber the word of the Supreme Being—to members only.

Shopping

Where?

The government-run Intur and Caracol boutiques in the major hotels have a wide selection, selling strictly for dollars, with prices that are not exorbitant but are not subject to bargaining either. Two other state-controlled outlets for handicrafts, musical instruments and clothes are Havana's Palacio de la Artesanía, on the corner of Cuba and Tacón streets, and the Fondo Cubano de Bienes Culturales, on Plaza Vieja. Bargaining is possible at the open-air market on Plaza de la Catedral. A flea market, Area de Vendadores por Cuenta Propia, is held daily at the corner of Máximo Gómez and Suárez. Varadero has two shopping malls—Centro Comercial Copey near the Siboney and Atabey hotels and Centro Comercial Caimán opposite Hotel Cuatro Palmas.

What?

To buy things that capture the atmosphere of Cuba, it's a good idea not to shop before you've gained a feeling for the place.

Cigars

In the dwindling world of tobacco smokers, there is still a place apart for the connoisseur of the hand-rolled Cuban cigar packed in a handsome cedarwood box. The leading brands come in sealed boxes of 25 cigars. In US dollars, the best range from the most expensive, Castro's favourite Cohiba Esplendidos ($300 per box in 1997) to the Montecristo No. 4 ($55). In between are the popular Partagás and Romeo y Julieta (both between $60 and $80). Beware of black-market cigars. Even when they are sold in sealed boxes with famous labels, they may be fakes.

Rum

Since the post-revolutionary departure of Bacardí to Puerto Rico, Cuba's best brand is Havana Club, founded in 1878 and distinguished by the Giraldilla statue on the label. Top of the range is seven-year-old brown Añejo, then five-year-old golden dry Carta de Oro and, for cocktails, three-year-old light, dry white Carta Blanca.

Clothes

The Cuban farm-worker's shirt, the light and airy pleated cotton *guayabera*, is suitable both for evening wear at the bar or for daytime sun protection on the beach. Dollar shops sell designer- 65

The best and worst of local art can be found on and around Havana's Plaza de la Catedral.

label garments of dubious authenticity. Revolutionary nostalgics and romantics buy Che Guevara posters and T-shirts or others bearing a raised fist with the colours of the Cuban flag and still proclaiming hopefully *Venceremos!* ("We shall win!").

Music

Cuban and Afro-Cuban rhythms are something you can take with you in the form of CDs (made under license in Canada for Egrem-Artex, the Cuban state recording company). The best introductory selections are: *Fiesta Cubana Guakiras*, several volumes of *Joyas de la Música Cubana* and *Antología de la Música Cubana*. Artex has its own shop in Havana, opposite the Habana Libre hotel in Vedado. You may also want to join in with authentic musical instruments, a *tres* guitar, a *maraca* rattle, a pair of *bongó* drums or at least a couple of *claves* rhythm sticks.

Art and Antiques

Modern paintings and sculpture and antiques from the Spanish colonial era can be of high quality, best purchased at galleries providing a receipt to permit export. In Havana, there are several around Plaza de la Catedral and near the Gran Teatro.

Dining Out

Cuban cuisine, whether Spanish creole or Afro-Cuban, does not claim any great gourmet delicacies, but there are some hearty and savoury meals to be had, mostly of pork and chicken. Whilst garlic and onions are common, hot spices or chili peppers are practically non-existent. Despite the abundance of fish in the Caribbean and Atlantic, Cubans themselves tend not to go for seafood dishes, but they are available for tourists.

Most hotels catering to large groups provide copious buffets with a mixture of Caribbean and international dishes. Selection in state-run restaurants outside the hotels may be meagre, depending on the ups and downs of the national economy. Menus are often only in Spanish.

The new factor, increasingly since their official authorization in 1995, is the *paladar*, the small private establishment offering good barbecued pork and chicken dishes and, clandestinely, sumptuous lobster and shrimp dinners. Payment is reasonable, in dollars only, but don't ask your hotel about them: the competition is not welcome.

To start with...

...you may find a fine shrimp soup, *sopa de camarones*, served with chopped onions, diced potatoes fresh cream and herbs. You may also be lucky to come across tiny but delicious Atlantic oysters, brought in to beach resorts from Isabela de Sagua on the north coast.

Main Course

A common feature of the Cuban table is simply chicken and rice (*arroz con pollo*), sometimes served with peas, chopped ham, olives and green bell peppers. Creole chicken (*pollo con salsa criolla*) has a garlic, tomato and onion sauce and is served with sweet corn. Barbecued chicken (*pollo barbacoa*) is usually accompanied by fried rice.

Roast meat (*carne asado*) is most often pork (*puerco*) or beef (*res*). From the Camagüey region comes a tasty *ajicao* stew combining pork, sweet potatoes, manioc and garlic.

Two very popular versions of a Caribbean staple are the Cuban *moros y cristianos*, black beans and rice, and the Haitian *congrí* 67

oriental, rice with red beans, brought in by French planters in the 19th century.

Lobster *(langosta)* and shrimps *(camarones)* are generally grilled and served plain or accompanied by a spicy tomato sauce *(enchilada)*.

Desserts

Cuba's Coppelia ice cream *(helado)* is much sought-after and sometimes scarce. It's at its best with a vanilla pudding *(natilla)*. Try fried ripe bananas with cinnamon and sugar *(plátano en tentación)* or plain caramel pudding *(flan)*. Rice pudding may be deliciously flavoured with cinnamon and green lime preserves.

Drinks

Rum, a distillation of the sugar-crop's finest molasses with water and yeast, has been made in Cuba since Spanish times. With the new distilleries of Havana, Cárdenas and Matanzas, a high-quality product was developed in the 19th century. Most cocktails are made with white rum; dark rum is coloured with caramel.

Cuba libre is with cola and lemon on the rocks; *Cuba bella* with grenadine, crème de menthe, lemon and crushed ice; *Daïquirí* with maraschino, lemon, sugar and crushed ice; *Mojito* with lime or lemon, fresh mint, soda, on the rocks; *Mary Pickford* with pine-

---

GOING BANANAS

Sweet or savoury, bananas are cooked in as many different ways as potatoes in Europe. The plantain banana is more properly a vegetable, fried or chopped into a meat stew. Green plantains are boiled, mashed and salted to make a tasty purée *(fufú)* served with roast pork or chicken. *Tostones* and *tachinos* are thick fried green banana chips. The thinner variety is known as *chicharitas*. Most potent of all is the banana daiquiri rum cocktail.

---

apple juice, crushed ice and grenadine; *Piña colada* with pineapple juice, coconut cream and crushed ice; and the *Zombie*, a killer blending three rums—old brown, mellow golden and young white—with lemon and orange juice, grenadine, fruit and crushed ice. You should also look out for some fine local liqueurs: chocolate mint, banana, triple sec, maraschino, pineapple and an egg liqueur, *Ponche Kuba*.

Coffee is excellent—strong and black *cafecito*, French-style strong coffee with hot milk *(café con leche)*. If you prefer it weak, you must ask for *café americano*.

Tap water is a risk. It's better to stick to bottled mineral water *(agua mineral)*.

Nightlife

There are some people who come to Cuba and never see it by the light of day. And still have a fine time. Even those who do not intend staying up all night and sleeping all day should enjoy one of the best sides of Cuban life and join the exuberant islanders in their singing, dancing and all-round party-going.

Nightclubs, bars, cabarets and discothèques abound in Havana, Varadero and Santiago de Cuba. You should know in advance that you cannot hope to combine an evening of good music and dancing with an early night. Many of the favourite nightspots do not really get started or even open before 10 p.m. and then go on to the wee small hours of the morning.

We guide you here to the best known places. Most are well established institutions, but on the fast-changing Cuban entertainment scene, some inevitably close, some change their names. However, one of the great pleasures of Cuba for the more adventurous is to stumble on an open-air party when the fun on a hot night has spilled out onto the street or beach. Strangers are almost always welcome, all the more so if they bring a good bottle of rum. These places you must find for yourself. Just follow the sound of the music.

HAVANA

Tropicana

Calle 72 N° 4504 y Calle 43
Marianao
Tel. 27 01 10
9 p.m.–2 a.m.; closed Mon
This huge nightclub, open-air in fair weather, is certainly the most famous in Cuba and perhaps in the whole Caribbean. A national institution since its opening in 1939, it is located at the south end of Vedado, quite far out in the city's western outskirts, but is served by shuttle-buses stopping at the major hotels. Reservations for either of the two shows (9.30 and 11.30 p.m.) are essential. Prices may seem steep, including transportation and one cocktail, but you get your money's worth. The floorshow is truly spectacular, with scores of gorgeous, extravagantly costumed dancers, male and female, strutting their stuff on the stage and snaking their way among the tables in an exotic setting of tropical vegeta-

tion. The atmosphere is quite as intoxicating as the freely flowing rum, tempting the most staid customers to get up on their chairs and dance.

Parisien

Hotel Nacional
Calle O, Vedado
Tel. 33 35 64
9 p.m.–2.30 a.m.; closed Thurs
The opulent cabaret is located in the hotel whose guests once ranged from Winston Churchill to Ava Gardner—and several less savoury but equally renowned American mafiosi such as Meyer Lansky. Before the Revolution, Frank Sinatra sang here. Today, you can enjoy a splashy floorshow, smaller in scale than the Tropicana (and priced more modestly), but just as lively, and then launch into your own salsa, rumba and mambo when the dance-floor is opened to disco music.

Copa Room

Hotel Riviera
Paseo y Malecón
Vedada
Tel. 33 40 51
9 p.m. to 3 a.m.; closed Tues
Replacing the legendary Palacio de la Salsa, the old hotel's nightclub has been refurbished to capture the glittering atmosphere of the 1950s. Under the old nickname of the famous Copacabana,

it has two floorshows, at 10 p.m. and midnight, with prices moderately expensive.

Café Cantante

Teatro Nacional de Cuba
Paseo y Calle 39
Plaza de la Revolución
Tel. 33 57 13
11 p.m.–4 a.m.
No frills here, but more modest prices, but the performance of Havana's most celebrated *son* and *salsa* groups such as Los Van Van and Charanga Habanera make this club in the basement of the national theatre a favourite nightspot for young Cubans. You may have to compete with long queues of Habaneros to get in, but it is well worth it for the high-octane ambience. Whether there is a concert or disco, people are dancing non-stop.

Delirio Habanero

Teatro Nacional de Cuba
Paseo y Calle 39
Plaza de la Revolución
10 p.m. to 2 a.m.
Despite its delirious name, this café bar upstairs in the national theatre has a more sedate atmosphere than most of the other clubs. It attracts mostly Cuban students and artists listening and occasionally dancing to the city's newest groups. The music is first class and the price of drinks very reasonable.

71

La Tropical

Avenida 41 y Calle 46
Playa
Open all night
every night

Located on the southern outskirts of town, this big open-air nightclub is without doubt Havana's hottest spot, where 9 out of 10 guests are Cubans. This is the place to learn the newest Latin American dances. To enjoy the uninhibited atmosphere to the full, but without unnecessary paranoia, leave your jewels and extra cash at the hotel.

La Zorra y el Curvo

Calle 23 N° 155, between
Calle N and O
Vedado
9 p.m.–4 a.m.

With an old bright red London telephone box for its entrance, "The Vixen and the Crow" presents the best in live Afro-Cuban and Latin American jazz in a modest but pleasant club atmosphere—for listening rather than dancing. Prices moderate.

VARADERO

Cabaret Continental

Hotel Internacional
Carretera Las Americas
Tel. 61 30 11
Closed Mon

The beach resort's huge and equally expensive counterpart to Havana's Tropicana, with a show at

10 p.m. followed by disco dancing. The floorshow is dazzling, the costumes awesomely daring.

La Cueva del Pirata

Carretera Las Morlas, km 11
Tel. 66 77 51
9 p.m.–3 a.m.; closed Sun

The "Pirate's Cave" provides a colourful setting for its 10 p.m. floorshow followed by boisterous disco dancing. Prices moderate.

Jardines Mediterraneo

Avenida 1ra y Calle 54
Tel. 61 24 60
8.30 p.m.–4 a.m.

Refreshingly old-fashioned ambience for its two floorshows, at 9 p.m. and 2 a.m. The traditional music is matched by Cuban food and drinks. Reasonable prices.

La Bamba

Hotel Tuxpan
Tel. 66 75 60
10 p.m. to 4 a.m.

Varadero's liveliest and most popular beachfront disco, with futuristic décor and videos. Moderate to expensive.

SANTIAGO DE CUBA

La Casa De La Trova

Calle José María Heredia
11.30 a.m.–1 a.m.; closed Mon

Located near the cathedral, this café is the home of Afro-Cuban music in its most traditional forms. Surrounded by photos of the Oriente region's best-loved musicians, concerts are staged throughout the day, in a pleasant lounge, the bar or—late at night —in the inner patio, for both dancing and listening.

La Casa De Las Tradiciones

Calle Rabi N° 154
Tivoli
7 p.m.–2 a.m.;
closed Tues, Sat and Sun

Strictly for aficionados of authentic Afro-Cuban music, in a home setting.

Tropicana

Autopista Nacional, km 1.5
Tel. 430 36
9 p.m.–3 a.m.

Santiago's giant namesake equivalent of Havana's hotspot is located 6 km northeast of the city centre. Extravagant stage-sets, spectacular lighting, music and costumes make the open-air floorshows (10 p.m. and 1 a.m.) worth the high prices.

Cabaret San Pedro del Mar

Carretera del Moreo, next to Hotel Balcón del Caribe

With its delightful open-air terrace, this moderately priced seafront nightclub 7 km southwest of town is more popular with Cubans than tourists. Guests dance both during the concerts and the post-show disco.

73

Sports

Revolutionary Cuba has always prided itself on its sporting prowess, performing exceptionally well in Olympic athletics and team sports. You can still see mementos from the Pan-American Games, hosted by Cuba in 1992. There are first-class facilities for the visitor, notably in water sports organized around the island's coasts by Marina Puertosol.

Swimming and Surfing

For family swimming, the long white sandy beaches at Varadero, Guardalavaca and on the Cayos are a sheer delight. Remember that the waters are calmer in the winter on the south and west coasts (November to April) and in summer on the north coast (May to September).

Wind-surfing equipment is available for rent at most resorts. Besides Varadero and Guardalavaca, the best conditions are at Cayo Largo and Marea del Portillo, the black-sand beach on the south coast of the Sierra Maestra. Surfers have to bring their own boards to enjoy the great waves brought in by the northeast trade winds on the Atlantic coast from December to April and, on the Caribbean coast, in August and September.

Diving

At Havana, Marina Hemingway, 20 km (12 miles) west of the city centre, provides good facilities and training courses for scuba diving, as do most of the major resorts. Aficionados home in on Cayo Coco and María La Gorda. For exploring underwater caves, try Varadero and Playa Girón.

Both Varadero (through Cubanáutica near the Kawama hotel) and Havana's Marina Hemingway rent out yachts for day trips or for overnight with lobster meals and drinks galore.

Fishing

The Gulf Stream creates conditions for deep-sea fishing at its best on the northwest coast—Havana, Varadero, Cayo Guillermo and Guardalavaca's Bahía de Naranjo for barracuda, sailfish, shark, swordfish, tuna and mackerel. For freshwater lake fishing for bass, perch and trout, try Pinar del Río's Laguna Grande and Morón's Laguna la Redonda (easy access by causeway from Cayo Coco).

Absolutely anything goes on Cuba's sandy beaches.

Horseback Riding

The beach resorts hire out horses by the hour, as does Havana's Parque Lenin. For longer treks, you might try the tourist ranches near Trinidad at Casa del Campesino or Los Molinos. Other good facilities in the interior are available in the Viñales valley and Pinar del Río.

Hiking

The most ambitious hiking trails are to be found in the Sierra Maestra national park, but there are also delightful rambles in the forests around the Gran Piedra and, in the west, Soroa and Viñales. In the absence of detailed trail-maps, it may be best to hire a local guide.

Golf

You will find an 18-hole course at Varadero's Las Américas club and nine holes at the Havana Golf Club. More are planned.

Spectator Sports

There is a superb atmosphere at the town's baseball stadium, where matches are held every day except Monday and Friday during the November-to-March season. Tickets are easy to obtain at the stadium and free of charge. Soccer, basketball and volleyball also attract enthusiastic crowds.

75

The Hard Facts

Airports
Most international flights serve Havana's José Martí Airport, Varadero and Santiago de Cuba. The terminals provide banking, car-hire and tourist information office services, in addition to duty-free shop, restaurant and snack bar facilities. There are bus and taxi links to town.

Climate
Caressed by the prevailing north-east trade winds, the island's climate is agreeably sub-tropical, most often around 25°C (77°F), rising to an average 28°C (82°F) in July and August and "dipping" to 22°C (71°F) in the coolest month, February. The east, especially the mountains, gets more rain than the west. The hurricane season is from June to November, most likely in September and October and more often in the west around Havana and Pinar del Río than in the east. Storm winds can reach 250 kph (156 mph). Swimmers take note: Caribbean waters are slightly warmer than the Atlantic.

Communications
Postal services, as almost everywhere these days, are very slow and unreliable. If you have urgent mail, ask your hotel about the international courier services available. The island's telephone services are problematic, though a phone card system is being progressively installed in the major tourist areas. Calls are best handled through your hotel, which also usually has fax facilities. Check the price first to avoid unpleasant surprises.

Crime
Cuba is much safer than other Latin American countries—and many places in North America. Pickpockets, however, work the tourist areas of Havana and the resort towns. A much sought-after item is your passport, so keep it well-protected. Prostitutes in hotel lobbies and street-corner hustlers (*jineteros*) are an inevitable offshoot of tourism and the island's economic difficulties, but beggars and anyone else that hassles you can be shooed off with a calm *"Por favor, no moleste"*— "Please, don't bother me."

Driving
The island has a well-developed network of roads, with a main highway linking Pinar del Río to Guantánamo, more than 1,120 km (700 miles) away, and several

good coastal highways between the resorts.

Driving is on the right. The rules follow Western European and North American norms and speed limits—50 kph (30 mph) in town, 90 kph (56 mph) on paved country highways, 100 kph (62 mph) on the Autopista Nacional.

To rent a car, you must be 21 or over, have a valid driver's licence and preferably an internationally accepted credit card (not drawing on a US bank).

Even when there is a shortage for Cubans, fuel is usually available to foreign tourists at 24-hour Servi-Cupet filling stations. Payment—as for tolls on major highways and the Cayos causeways—is in dollars only.

Electric Current

The current is mostly 110 volts, 60 cycles, with US-style flat-pin plugs, but European-run hotels are increasingly equipped with 220-volt current and round-pin plugs, so be prepared with an adaptor for both.

Emergencies

Most problems can be handled at your hotel desk. Telephone number for police is **116**, for fire **115**, and for ambulance **118**, Spanish-speaking only. Consular help is there only for critical situations, lost passports or worse, *not* for lost cash or plane tickets.

Essentials

Travel light, especially as far as clothing is concerned. You won't need much formal wear. Pack a sun-hat and add a sweater for cool evenings. Good walking shoes are vital, especially for the mountains, and sandals or moccasins for the beach. Bring along sun-block, insect repellent and a pocket torch (flashlight) in case of electricity cuts.

Formalities

Apart from a passport, still valid for at least six months after you enter Cuba, you should obtain a tourist card *(tarjeta de turista)*, usually provided by your travel agency or tour operator. Keep it safe during your stay as you will need to hand it in when leaving. (US citizens are discouraged only by their own government, not at all by Cuban authorities, who give them a warm welcome if they come equipped with an appropriate *tarjeta de turista* and will not put a potentially embarrassing stamp in their passports.)

One item that Cuban customs officers are on the look-out for is cigars, so if you buy them, be sure to keep your official receipts. The export limit is 200 cigars per person. Note that US customs will confiscate Cuban cigars, but you do at least have the right to rip them apart rather than let the officials smoke them in secret!)

77

Health

Apart from minor stomach upsets from change of diet, the big health hazard in Cuba is the sun. Watch out for sunstroke, heat exhaustion and dehydration. Stick to the shade, wear a hat, use a good sun-screen, drink plenty of bottled mineral water.

Cuba's doctors, hospital staff and dentists throughout the island have excellent training. First visits to public hospitals are free and very cheap thereafter. For emergencies, make sure your health insurance covers holiday illnesses. If you expect to need prescription medicines, take your own as you may not find the exact equivalent on the spot.

Language

Spanish is the national language. Tour guides and some hotel staff speak English, French or German. If you try Russian as a joke, people may not laugh.

Media

The official Communist Party organ in Spanish, *Granma*, is also the national newspaper, more popular than you might expect, particularly because paper shortages have cut back other publications. A weekly press review, *Granma Internacional*, is published in English, French and German. Big hotels receive international cable TV via satellite.

Money

US dollars are well entrenched as the accepted currency for foreign tourists. The convertible *peso*, which divides into 100 *centavos*, has an official exchange rate one-to-one with the US dollar. The *peso cubano*, 20 to the dollar, will be of no use to you except perhaps for bus tickets, local phone calls and stamps. Banknotes range from 1 to 100 *pesos* and coins from 1 to 50 *centavos*. Change back your *pesos* before leaving the country.

International credit cards and traveller's cheques are accepted as long as they are not negotiable through US banks, but not Eurocheques. Cash is preferred.

Opening Hours

The following times are given as a general guide, some of them being subject to variations.

Banks open on weekdays from 8.30 a.m. to 12 p.m. and 1.30 to 3 p.m.; Saturday 8 to 10 a.m.

Shops are open Monday to Saturday 9.30 a.m. to 12.30 p.m. and 2 to 5 p.m. They sometimes close later in Havana.

Pharmacies open from 8 a.m. to 8 p.m.

Main post offices open Monday to Saturday 8 a.m. to 6 p.m., sometimes later in big cities.

Museums open Tuesday to Saturday from 9 a.m. to 5 p.m. and Sunday 8 a.m. to noon.

Photography

You are likely to find only colour-print film available in Cuba, and more expensive than back home, so stock up before you arrive. Choose film speeds for the brilliant Caribbean light. Most museums and public monuments allow cameras, but usually charge an extra fee, with restrictions on the use of flash. Avoid photographing factories, airports and naval bases.

Public Holidays

Most shops, offices and museums are closed on the following dates:

January 1	Liberation Day
May 1	Labour Day
July 25–27	Celebration of the National Rebellion
October 10	Day of Cuban Culture
December 25	Christmas

Public Transport

Since the bus service has been crippled by fuel shortages and lack of spare parts for vehicles, your best bet is the really good national train network or, for longer distances, domestic flights. The only functioning railway in the Caribbean covers nearly 5,000 km (over 3,000 miles) of track, linking all the major towns from Pinar del Río via Havana to Santiago de Cuba. Tourists pay very reasonable fares in dollars; the seating is old-fashioned but comfortable. Coffee and sandwiches are served from station platforms along the route.

Taxis and Bicy-Taxis

There are plenty of taxis available at the airport and major hotels; negotiate the fare before getting in. If necessary, have someone from your hotel make the conditions clear. Bicycle-taxis with the rider pedalling in front of a couple of passengers are also plentiful. Again prices should be determined before you get in.

Time Difference

GMT–5, the same as Eastern Standard Time, with daylight saving time from April to September, when it is GMT–4.

Tipping

Discouraged by orthodox revolutionary ideology, tipping is becoming a habit again with the growth of tourism. Hotel and restaurant staff appreciate direct tipping rather than having it included in the overall bill—again, dollars only.

Toilets

Use the public toilets in the major hotels—marked *Señores* or *Hombres* for men, *Señoras* or *Mujeres* for women—as many restaurants do not have facilities and do not necessarily supply toilet paper.

INDEX

Arawak legacy 60
Architecture 60
Banes 56
Baracoa 55
Bay of Pigs 44
Bayamo 53–54
Camagüey 46
Cárdenas 36–37
Carnival 60–61
Carpentier, Alejo 61
Castro, Fidel 13ff., 24, 43ff.
Cayo Coco 59
– Guillermo 59
– Largo 59
– Romano 59
Cienfuegos 42–43
Cigars 25–26, 28, 40
Cojímar 33
Comandancia de la Plata 54
Cueva del Indio 39–40
– de San Miguel 40
El Cobre 52–53
Finca la Vigía 32
Gran Piedra 51–52
Guantánamo 54–55
Guardalavaca 55–56
Guevara, Ernesto Che 13ff., 26, 32, 43–44
Gutiérrez Alea, Tomás 61
Havana 17–33
  Churches 23–25
  Fortresses 31–32
  Museums 18–19, 20–23, 25, 27–28, 30
  Outskirts 31–33

Parque Lenin 33
Hemingway, Ernest 12, 23, 32
Holguín 55
Isla de la Juventud 57–59
Lam, Wilfredo 61
Malecón 28
Mariel 38
Martí, José 10, 25, 27
Matanzas 37–38
Mogote dos Hermanas 39
Music 61–63
Pico Turquino 54
Pinar del Río 40–41
Pinares del Mayarí 56
Playa Ancón 45–46
Playa Bailen 41
Playa María La Gorda 41
Playas del Este 33
Religion 63–64
San Diego de los Baños 39
Sancti Spíritus 46
Santa Clara 43–44
Santiago de Cuba 49–51
Sierra Maestra 54
Soroa 39
Tobacco Country 41
Trinidad 44–45
Tropicana 70
Valle de Los Ingenios 46
Varadero 35–36
Vedado 28–31
Viñales Valley 39–40

GENERAL EDITOR:
  Barbara Ender-Jones
EDITOR:
  Amanda Hopkins
LAYOUT:
  Luc Malherbe
PHOTO CREDITS:
  Mireille Vautier, front cover;
  Jacques Straesslé, back cover, pp. 16, 29;
  Hémisphères/Gotin, p. 1;
  Hémisphères/Frances, pp. 2, 21, 22, 32, 34, 47, 56, 72, 75;
  Rainer Hackenberg, pp. 6, 24, 48, 52, 58;
  Neil Setchfield, pp. 14, 43, 66;
  Christine Osborne Pictures, pp. 27, 68
MAPS:
  Elsner & Schichor

Printed in Switzerland
Gessler/Sion (CTF)
Edition 2000–2001

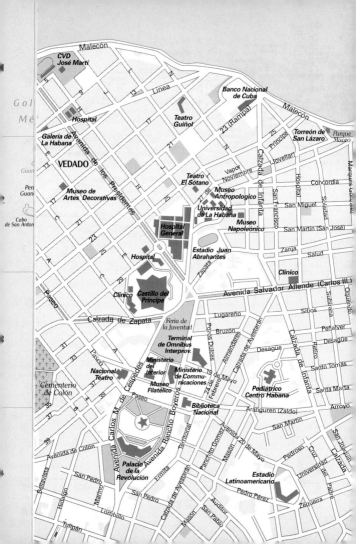

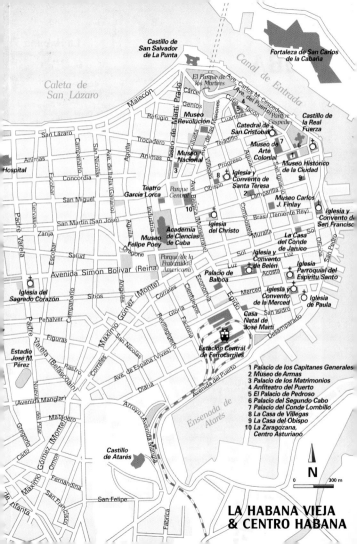

Castillo de San Salvador de La Punta

Fortaleza de San Carlos de la Cabaña

Canal de Entrada

Caleta de San Lázaro

El Parque de los Mártires

Ave. Carlos M. Céspedes (Ave. del Puerto)

Malecón

Cárcel

Genios

Castillo de la Real Fuerza

San Lázaro

Refugio

Museo Revolución

Catedral de San Cristóbal

Castillo de la Real Fuerza

Animas

Trocadero

Museo de Arte Colonial

Museo Histórico de la Ciudad

Hospital

Concordia

Museo Nacional

Iglesia y Convento de Santa Teresa

San Miguel

Teatro García Lorca

Parque Central

Museo Carlos J. Finlay

Iglesia y Convento de San Francisco

San Martín (San José)

Academia de Ciencias de Cuba

Iglesia del Christo

La Casa del Conde de Jaruco

Zanja

Museo Felipe Poey

Iglesia y Convento de Belén

Salud

Parque de la Fraternidad Americana

Iglesia Parroquial del Espíritu Santo

Avenida Simón Bolívar (Reina)

Palacio de Balboa

Iglesia del Sagrado Corazón

Sitios

Iglesia y Convento de la Merced

Iglesia de Paula

Peñalver

Gloria

Casa Natal de José Martí

Figuras

Estadio José M. Pérez

Estación Central de Ferrocarriles

(Avenida Manglar)

Matadero

Ensenada de Atarés

Castillo de Atarés

San Felipe

1 Palacio de los Capitanes Generales
2 Museo de Armas
3 Palacio de los Matrimonios
4 Anfiteatro del Puerto
5 El Palacio de Pedroso
6 Palacio del Segundo Cabo
7 Palacio del Conde Lombillo
8 La Casa de Villegas
9 La Casa del Obispo
10 La Zaragozana, Centro Asturiano

N

0   300 m

LA HABANA VIEJA & CENTRO HABANA